The

QUOTABLE
PARENT

Praise for *The Quotable Parent*

"Informative, entertaining, and meaningful . . . a treasure of quotes from our greatest teachers, our parents."

Chester Elton
NY Times best-selling author of *The Carrot Principle*

"Joel Weiss has always had the ability of recognizing good thinking where he saw it. The Quotable Parent captures just about all the good thinking he has collected over the years. Besides being a great read, it will save you the time of having to wade through Bartlett's Famous Quotations."

Jack Trout
World famous marketing strategist and author

"It's a great book to use to impart the wisdom of the ages to yourself and your children. The principles outlined in this book through the authors' commentary and quotes can be used throughout one's lifetime."

Will Gooden
Former VP International Finance of Burger King Corporation

"This father and son share the insights of many writers which are cleverly woven together to create an uplifting book. As a parent myself, I find this to be a source of wisdom and motivation, but you do not have to be a parent to enjoy it. Thank you for coming up with the perfect gift for the people I care about."

Karen Kidd
Mother, house wife, artist, and charity activist

"The Quotable Parent is a marvelous compendium that is entertaining as it is thought provoking and a valuable desk top companion for those who communicate regularly with the public. Joel Weiss has married up his wisdom and world experience with his son John's generational sensitivity and contemporary flair to hand pick, and thoughtfully organize, the best of history's light hearted and serious expressions for everyday use. No home, school or business should be without a copy.

Charles Olcott
Former President of Burger King Corporation

"Grab a pencil before you start reading this wonderful book. You'll want to write down many of these marvelous quotes."

Al Ries
Author of *War in the Boardroom*

"What a great reservoir of ageless ideas and observations to draw from. The author has made it easy for a parent to find and use the quotes that are needed for meaningful dialogues during a child's formative years."

Antony A. Brilakis
Retired small business owner

"The book captures the power of quotes and the profound impact through a simple few words but such strong messages. As a parent and a leader this book grabbed me from the Introduction to the conclusion and forced me to reflect on all aspects of my personal and professional life like never before. The authors do such a wonderful job of capturing both historical and modern messages that benefit anyone who reads the book. You won't put it down once you start!"

John Wurzburger
President of Performance Fibers

"This book delivers what it promises, to motivate, educate, inform and give the reader a useful tool and companion that one will refer to often. The quotes are powerful, regardless of the subject. It will become a permanent addition to my reference library. "

Tom Rea
Former SVP and Corporate Officer of Fisher Scientific International Inc.
and Founder of Executive Assessment Group LLC

"I found this book and the way the quotes were written to be inspiring and thought provoking during these very difficult times. These quotes are not just for parents and children. We are all someone's child, parent, grandparent, spouse, lover or friend and these quotes stand the test of time."

Stefan Sleigh
Son, husband, father, friend, and CEO

Advice from the Greatest Minds in History

The
QUOTABLE
PARENT

JOEL WEISS AND JOHN WEISS

Published by Familius LLC, www.familius.com

Familius books are available at special discounts for bulk purchases for sales promotions, family or corporate use. Special editions, including personalized covers, excerpts of existing books, or books with corporate logos, can be created in large quantities for special needs. For more information, contact Premium Sales at 801-552-7298 or email specialmarkets@familius.com

Library of Congress Catalog-in-Publication Data

2012951096

pISBN: 978-1-938301-28-5
eISBN: 978-1-938301-27-8

Printed in the United States of America

Book design by Maggie Wickes
Edited by Edith Songer
Cover design by Andrea C. Copper

First Edition

TABLE OF CONTENTS

Introduction

"Many receive advice, only the wise profit from it."

Cyrus the Great, 600–529BC

Quotes have always been a great tool for learning, motivation, and inspiration. A quote captures valuable information or insight and in a few words can tell the whole story.

British prime minister and author Benjamin Disraeli wrote, "The wisdom of the wise and the experience of the ages are perpetuated by quotes."

We are always impressed when we see how well the words of these famous people have passed the test of time. From Socrates in 460 BC to today's world, the quotes still carry the same message and meaning.

This book presents quotes to help parents to be better parents. As well, it is for their children who may be old enough to understand the meaning of these words. We believe that these valuable words could have a positive effect on all their lives.

It is presented in a simple format—the quotes are grouped into chapters by subjects such as Attitude and Leadership. There are also biographies for selected quote authors in a separate section at the end, listed in alphabetical order.

The quotes have been selected based on our real life experiences and real everyday events and problems. We believe they will be important to the reader. They are educational and motivational, filled with common sense and often humor. We think you'll find that you can use them in everyday events and life.

I have met many people and I have found that they see the value and convenience of using quotes as a way to think, learn, and teach in everyday situations. I have always been impressed and captivated by the power of these words spoken by the leaders of the world, past and present. And I believe these words can continue to guide our vision well into the future. These quotes have been gathered from people of all ages and occupations and locations in the world. From them we can take messages that have meaning now in our time. We address the parents because their job is so important and they have so many responsibilities today.

Many of my associates use quotes on an everyday basis; in letters, speeches, conversations—any way they communicate—to make their thinking clearly understood and also memorable. You will remember some of the short, to-the-point sayings like, "Early to bed and early to rise makes a man healthy, wealthy and wise." Or, "Haste makes waste." So short and yet these are messages that people remember all their lives. In my own experience it is often through quotes that I became interested in the authors' lives. Learning the words of people like Mark Twain, Will Rogers—the list goes on and on— leads you to read their biographies. Your children will be led to read some famous person's biography and will be better for it. Many a successful person has recommended learning from the lives of others.

I am always impressed with quotes that take you to another era, even BC, and yet the words are still meaningful. Here are a few that I picked:

"Many receive advice, only the wise profit from it."
Cyrus the Great, 600–529BC

"Are you really listening or are you waiting your turn to talk?"
Robert Montgomery, 1807–1855

"Genius is divine perseverance. Genius I cannot have but perseverance all can have."
Woodrow Wilson, 1856–1934

"There's no trick to being a humorist when you have the whole government working for you."
Will Rogers, 1879–1935

"You can tell the character of every man when you see how he accepts praise."
Seneca, 4 BC–65 AD

When you read quotes you can learn so much and find the best words to present a thought or idea. It's no wonder that we use quotes in our speeches, letters, conversations, and any form of communication. You can remember quotes and with that, a message that can be good advice.

In this time of high unemployment, here is some good advice from Theodore Roosevelt, our 26th president:

> *"Whenever you are asked if you can do a job, tell them, 'Certainly I can!' Then get busy and find out how to do it."*

Wherever possible we have tried to include information on quote authors, dates, occupation, honors and any information that we could find, though that was not always possible.

The quotes were gathered from many sources such as the internet, newspapers, public writing, all available to the public. We have also learned from biographies, research, and history in general about the authors and their times. I believe we can say that the quotes are so content rich that they speak for themselves.

We hope you enjoy this book and find it to be inspiring as well as interesting, motivational, and educational for you and your family.

Joel Weiss and John Weiss

FAMILY AND
FRIENDS

"And say my glory was I had such friends."

William Butler Yeats, 1865–1939

It starts early with your family. And this stabilizes life and prepares you for the future. Others may not have the benefit of this stable background and that also shapes their lives. Remember, you get what you give. If you have been neglected and shown little or no love, you are likely to pass this on to others.

The stability, character, love, and caring you see on a regular basis help to make you who you are and will become.

> *"Warmth, kindness, and friendship are the most yearned for commodities in the world. The person who can provide them will never be lonely."*
>
> Ann Landers, 1918–2002

Humor is also a vital ingredient in helping you through life and is essential in how you deal with other people. Having a sense of humor and being able to see the funny things in life can make you more equipped to deal with life and be a better parent. Many of the quotes in this chapter are humorous with a touch of truth.

> *"By the time a man realizes that maybe his father was right, he usually has a son who thinks he's wrong."*
> Charles Wadsworth

Remember the value of friendship is a key to success and happiness. We all need the support of friends with whom we can share our thoughts, ideas, ambitions, and problems.

> *"Family isn't about whose blood you have. It's about who you care about."*
> Trey Parker, 1969– and Matt Stone, 1971–

There are groups of people who identify themselves as family when in fact they are close friends but their commitment to each other can be as great as or greater than blood relatives. People basically want to be with and help other people.

No one succeeds in business and life alone. Success comes mostly as the result of a strong support team. Families that have not provided love and caring have essentially abandoned their children and if the children later achieve success and happiness, it is more likely through strong friends.

The most I
can do
for my friend
is simply to
be his friend.

Henry David Thoreau, 1817–1863

"Parents can only give good advice but the forming of a person's character lies in their own hands."

Anne Frank, 1929–1945

"Man's best possession is a sympathetic wife."

Euripides, 484–406 BC

"There's only one way to have a happy marriage and as soon as I learn what it is I'll get married again."

Clint Eastwood, 1930–

"The concept of two people living together for twenty-five years without having a cross word suggests a lack of spirit only to be admired in sheep."

Alan Patrick Herbert, 1890–1971

"Action, not words, is the true criterion for the attachment of friends."

George Washington, 1732–1799

"And say my glory was I had such friends."

William Butler Yeats, 1865–1939

"The central struggle of parenthood is to let our hopes for our children outweigh our fears."

Ellen Goodman, 1943–

"My toughest fight was with my first wife."

Muhammad Ali, 1942–

"To the soul, there is hardly anything more healing than friendship."

Thomas Moore, 1779–1852

"Friends are an aid to the young, to guard them from error; to the elderly, to attend to their wants and to supplement their failing power of action; to those in the prime of life, to assist them to noble deeds."

Aristotle, 384–322 BC

"My mother had a great deal of trouble with me, but I think she enjoyed it."

Mark Twain, 1835–1910

"The thing that impresses me the most about America is the way parents obey their children."

Edward VIII, 1894–1972

"The reason grandparents and grandchildren get along so well is that they have a common enemy."

Sam Levenson, 1911–1980

"Sooner or later we all quote our mother."

Bern Williams, 1929–2003

"There's sort of a cliché about parents, that they believe that their children are the most beautiful children in the world. But the thing is, what no one really talks about, is the fact that they all really believe it."

Heather Armstrong, 1975–

"A mother is not a person to lean on but a person to make leaning unnecessary."

Dorothy Parker, 1879–1958

"This is part of the essence of motherhood, watching your kid grow into her own person and not being able to do anything about it. Otherwise children would be nothing more than pets."

Heather Armstrong, 1975–

Grown-ups never
understand anything for themselves,
and it is tiresome for
children
to be
always and forever
explaining things to them.

Antoine de Saint-Exupery, 1900–1944

"A family is a unit composed not only of children but of men, women, an occasional animal, and the common cold."

Ogden Nash, 1902–1971

"Marriage is a great institution but I'm not ready for an institution yet."

Mae West, 1892–1980

"The most important thing she'd learned over the years was that there was no way to be a perfect mother and a million ways to be a good one."

Jill Churchill

"Call it a clan, call it a network, call it a tribe, call it a family; whatever you call it, whoever you are, you need one."

Jane Howard, 1923–

"There was a time when we expected nothing of our children but obedience, as opposed to the present, when we expect everything of them but obedience."

Anatole Broyard, 1920–1990

"Human beings are the only creatures that allow their children to come back home."

Bill Cosby, 1937–

"People who get nostalgic about childhood were obviously never children."

Bill Watterson, 1958–

"Facing a mirror you see merely your own countenance, facing your child you finally understand how everyone else has seen you."

Daniel Raeburn

"If your parents never had children, chances are you won't either."

Dick Cavett, 1936–

"The best way to keep children home is to make the home atmosphere pleasant and let the air out of the tires."

Dorothy Parker, 1893–1967

"The art of mothering is to teach the art of living to children."

Elaine Heffner

You know that
children are
growing up
when they
start asking
questions
that have
answers.

John J. Plomp,

"My mother loved children; she would have given anything if I had been one."

Groucho Marx, 1890–1977

"It is not giving children more that spoils them; it is giving them more to avoid confrontation."

John Gray, 1957–

"I love being married. It's so great to find that one special person you want to annoy for the rest of your life."

Rita Rudner, 1953–

"Your parents they gave you your life, but now and then they try to give you their life."

Chuck Palahniuk 1962–

"When I meet a man I ask myself, is this the man I want my children to spend their weekends with?"

Rita Rudner, 1953–

"The first half of our lives is ruined by our parents and the second half by our children."

Clarence Darrow, 1857–1938

"Always get married early in the morning. That way, if it doesn't work out, you haven't wasted a whole day."

Mickey Rooney, 1920–

"If you ever start feeling like you have the goofiest, craziest, most dysfunctional family in the world, all you have to do is go to a state fair, because five minutes at the fair, you'll be going, 'You know, we're alright. We are dang near royalty.'"

Jeff Foxworthy, 1958–

"We were happily married for eight months. Unfortunately, we were married for four and a half years."

Nick Faldo, 1957–

"Never have children, only grandchildren."

Gore Vidal, 1925–

"Parents were invented to make children happy by giving them something to ignore."

Ogden Nash, 1902–1971

HUMOR AND LIFE

"Humor is by far the most significant activity of the human brain."

Edward De Bono, 1933–

Humor is an essential part of life that brings and keeps people together. I feel for those who have not been introduced to humor and the funny things that life can bring. Your children will be happier and more understanding of others if they have a sense of humor. Why do you think so many successful TV shows and movies have been comedies?

Mark Twain, one of our greatest masters of humor, said, "Humor is the greatest thing, the saving thing. The minute it crops up, all our irritations and resentments slip away, and a sunny spirit takes their place."

He has been gone for a long time but he is still read and known worldwide. He is one of several who brought humor into our lives and his influence on us has no expiration date.

Another great quote about humor:

> *"Happiness is having a large, loving, caring, close-knit family in another city."*
>
> —George Burns, 1896–1996

He was one of the greatest comedians who loved life and humor. He lived to be 100 years old and worked as a comedian and actor to the end.

Still another great humorist and philosopher was Will Rogers, who said:

> *"There is no trick to being a humorist when you have the whole government working for you."*

Humor plays a big role in our lives and always will.

Among those whom I like or admire, I can find no $\frac{\text{common}}{\text{denominator}}$,

but among those whom I love, all of them make me laugh.

W.H. Auden, 1907–1973

"If you don't learn to laugh at trouble, you won't have anything to laugh at when you're old."

Edgar Watson Howe, 1853–1937

"I am not young enough to know everything."

Oscar Wilde, 1854–1900

"Suppose you were an idiot. And suppose you were a member of Congress . . . But then I repeat myself."

Mark Twain, 1835–1910

"Most turkeys taste better the day after, my mother's tasted better the day before."

Rita Rudner, 1953–

"The most remarkable thing about my mother is that for thirty years she served the family nothing but leftovers. The original meal has never been found."

Calvin Trillen, 1935–

"The future, according to some scientists, will be exactly like the past, only far more expensive."

John Sladek, 1938–2000

Humor
is by far the
most significant
activity
of the
human brain.

Edward De Bono, 1933–

You don't
stop laughing
because you
grow old.
You
grow old
because you
stop laughing.

Michael Pritchard

"Humor is also a way of saying something serious."

T. S. Eliot, 1888–1965

"Wit makes its own welcome and levels all distinctions. No dignity, no learning, no force of character, can make any stand against good wit."

Ralph Waldo Emerson, 1803–1882

"Some editors are failed writers, but so are most writers."

T. S. Eliot, 1888–1965

"Boyhood, like measles, is one of those complaints which a man should catch young and have done with, for when it comes in middle life it is apt to be serious."

P. G. Wodehouse, 1881–1975,

"I can win an argument on any topic, against any opponent. People know this and steer clear of me at parties. Often as a sign of their respect, they don't even invite me."

Dave Barry, 1947–

"You can only be young once but you can always be immature."

Dave Barry, 1947–

"My parents only had one argument in forty-five years. It lasted forty-three years."

Cathy Ladman, 1959–

"My idea of an agreeable person is someone who agrees with me."

Benjamin Disraeli, 1804–1881

"Youth is a wonderful thing. What a crime to waste it on children."

George Bernard Shaw, 1856–1950

"A sense of humor is part of the art of leadership, of getting along with people, of getting things done."

Dwight David Eisenhower, 1890–1969

To end this section about Humor, here are some simple puns:

Those who jump off a bridge in Paris are in seine.

A man's home is his castle, in a manor of speaking.

Shotgun wedding: a case of wife or death.

A hangover is the wrath of grapes.

Does the name Pavlov ring a bell?

Reading while sunbathing makes you well red.

When two egotists meet it's an I for an I.

What's the definition of a will? (It's a dead giveaway.)

A lot of money is tainted; it taint yours and it taint mine.

He had a photographic memory that was never developed.

A plateau is a high form of flattery.

Once you've seen one shopping center, you've seen a mall.

You feel stuck with your debt if you can't budge it.

ATTITUDE

"Morale and attitude are the fundamental ingredients to success."

Bud Wilkinson, 1916–1994

Attitude is defined as a state of mind. It is how you feel about everything. You've heard of having "a positive attitude" or "a good attitude" but also of having "a bad attitude" or "a poor attitude." A positive and friendly attitude with everyone in a genuine way will work wonders. You get what you give in life.

Norman Vincent Peale, a religious leader and writer, said:

> *"If your enthusiasm is infectious, stimulating, and attractive to others, they will love you for it. They will go for you and with you."*

You undoubtedly have known people with positive attitudes and most likely they have been successful. They get things done and do the right things.

Attitude is the key; never underestimate its power. Be optimistic, polite, sincere, and comfortable in social situations. Combine this with good work and you will increase the probability of your success. People will give back what they receive. When you are positive, happy, optimistic, and polite you will likely be treated the same way by others.

Developing what you do well will lead you to happiness. This is all another way to state the adage "If you can make a living doing what you love to do, you will never work another day in your life."

This chapter is full of excellent quotes on attitude that can help you as a parent and can equally help your children. Generally speaking, these quotes will improve your outlook on life and help your children to see what is important for their success.

Of course, a person's attitude can also be negative. Here are a couple of quotes that tell this story in a memorable way:

> *"It's wise to remember that anger is just one letter short of danger."*
>
> Sam Ewing, 1920–2001

> *"'I lose my temper but it's all over in a minute,' said one student. 'So is the hydrogen bomb,' I replied, 'but think of the damage it produces.'"*
>
> George Sweeting

Greet every person you meet
cheerfully
and
enthusiastically.
Nobody can fake
cheerfulness
and
enthusiasm
very long. You'll either
quit trying or improve
your outlook.

Nido Qubein, 1948–

"Morale and attitude are the fundamental ingredients to success."

Bud Wilkinson, 1916–1994

"The riches of life, the love and joy and exhilaration of life can be found only with an upward look. This is an exciting world. It's cram-packed with opportunity. Great moments wait around every corner."

Richard M. DeVos, 1926–

"Keep your face in the sunshine and you can never see the shadow."

Helen Keller, 1880–1968

"Watch your manner of speech if you wish to develop a peaceful state of mind. Start each day by affirming peaceful, contented, and happy attitudes and your days will tend to be pleasant and successful."

Norman Vincent Peale, 1898–1993

"A strong positive mental attitude will create more miracles than any wonder drug."

Patricia Neal, 1926–2010

"I have learned from experience that the greater part of our happiness or misery depends on our disposition and not our circumstances."

Martha Washington, 1732–1802

"Exude happiness and you will feel it back a thousand times."

Joan Lunden, 1950–

"There is a difference between happiness and wisdom: he that thinks he is the happiest man is really so, but he that thinks himself the wisest is generally the greatest fool."

Francis Bacon, 1561–1626

"Contentment comes not so much from great wealth as from few wants."

Epictetus 55–135 AD

"Develop an attitude of gratitude, and give thanks for everything that happens to you, knowing that every step forward is a step toward achieving something bigger and better than your current situation."

Brian Tracy, 1944–

Anything
you
are good at
contributes
to your
happiness.

Bertram Russell, 1872–1970

"Man only likes to count his troubles, but he does not count his joys."

Fyodor Dostoevsky, 1821–1881

"Worry affects the circulation, the heart, the glands, the whole nervous system, and profoundly affects the health. I have never known a man who died from over work, but many who have died from anxiety."

Dr. Charles W. Mayo, 1819–1911

"Remember no one can make you feel inferior without your consent."

Eleanor Roosevelt, 1884–1962

"Anger: an acid that can do more harm to the vessel in which it is stored than to anything on which it is poured."

Marcus Annaeus Seneca, 55 BC–40 AD

"Anger blows out the lamp of the mind. In the examination of a great and important question, everyone should be serene, slow pulsed, and calm."

Robert Green Ingersoll, 1833–1899

"Nothing in life is more remarkable than unnecessary anxiety which we endure and generally create ourselves."

Benjamin Disraeli, 1804–1881

"Being rich isn't about money. Being rich is a state of mind. Some of us, no matter how much money we have, will never be free enough to take time to stop and eat the heart of a watermelon. And some of us will be rich without ever being more than one paycheck ahead of the game."

Harvey B. Mackay, 1932–

GENEROSITY

"No act of kindness, no matter how small, is ever wasted."

Aesop, 620–560 BC

This is another trait that is an action for the good. Being generous to others can do nothing but good. I believe that every quote in this chapter is a brilliant choice of words that makes generosity more meaningful.

> *"The charity that is a trifle to us can be precious to others."*
>
> Homer, 8th century BC

> *"The best portion of a good man's life is his little nameless, unremembered acts of kindness and love."*
> William Wordsworth, 1770–1850

This chapter will make you feel good about the meaning of generosity and its importance to the whole world. It all starts from the family and what you learned growing up.

"Men exist for the sake of one another."
Marcus Aurelius, AD 121–180

Helping others is always the right thing to do. Whatever age you may be, think of the people that have helped you along the way and those you will help when the opportunity arises in the future.

Kindness is

more than deeds. It is an attitude, an expression, a look, a touch. It is anything that lifts another person.

C. Neil Strait, 1934–2003

"Three things in human life are important: the first is to be kind; the second is to be kind; and the third is to be kind."

Henry James, 1843–1916

"Let us not be satisfied with just giving money. Money is not enough; money can be got; but they need your hearts to love them."

Mother Teresa, 1910–1997

"I prefer to be remembered for what I have done for others, not for what others have done for me."

Thomas Jefferson, 1743–1826

"You must give some time to your fellow men, even if it's a little thing, do something for others, something for which you get no pay but the privilege of doing it."

Albert Schweitzer, 1875–1965

"My life belongs to the whole community, and as long as I live, it is my privilege to do for it whatever I can."

George Bernard Shaw, 1856–1950

"As simple as it sounds, we all must try to be the best person we can be; by making the best choices, by making the most of the talents we've been given."

Mary Lou Retton, 1968–

"No duty is more urgent than returning thanks."

St. Ambrose, 339–397

"A hundred times every day I remind myself that my inner and outer life depend on the labors of other men, living and dead, and that I must exert myself in order to give in the same measure I have received and am still receiving."

Albert Einstein, 1879–1955

"There never was a person who did anything worth doing, who did not receive more than he gave."

Henry Ward Beecher, 1813–1887

"I discovered a long time ago that if I helped people get what they wanted, I would always get what I wanted, and never had to worry."

Anthony Robbins, 1960–

Kindness
is a language
which the
deaf can hear
and the
blind can see.

Mark Twain, 1835–1910

"No person was ever honored for what he received. Honor has been the reward for what he gave."

Calvin Coolidge, 1872–1933

"Darkness cannot drive out darkness; only light can do that. Hate cannot drive out hate; only love can do that."

Martin Luther King Jr., 1929–1968

"Believe, when you are most unhappy, that there is something for you to do in the world. So long as you can sweeten another's pain, life is not all in vain."

Helen Keller, 1880–1968

"Blessed are those who give without remembering. And blessed are those who take without forgetting."

Bernard Meltzer, 1916–1998

"The greatest good you can do for another is not just to share your riches, but to reveal to him his own."

Benjamin Disraeli, 1804–1881

"If you treat an individual as he is, he will remain as he is. But if you treat him as if he were what he ought to be and could be, he will become what he ought to be and could be."

Johann Wolfgang von Goethe, 1749–1832

"Correction does much. But encouragement does more. Encouragement after censure is as the sun after the shower."

Johann Wolfgang Von Goethe, 1749–1832

"You have it easily within your power to increase the sum total of this world's happiness. How? By giving a few words of sincere appreciation to someone who is lonely or discouraged. Perhaps you will forget tomorrow the kind words you say today, but the recipient may cherish them over a lifetime."

Dale Carnegie, 1888–1955

"Flatter me and I may believe you, criticize me and I might not like you, ignore me and I may not forgive you, encourage me and I may not forget you."

William Arthur Ward, 1921–1994

When I first open
my eyes upon the
morning meadows
and look out upon
a beautiful world,
I thank God that I
am alive.

Ralph Waldo Emerson, 1803–1882

No act of *kindness,* no matter how *small,* is ever wasted.

Aesop, 620–560 BC

"Constant kindness can accomplish much. As the sun makes ice melt, kindness causes misunderstanding, mistrust and hostility to evaporate."

Albert Schweitzer, 1875–1965

"Only a life lived in the service to others is worth living."

Albert Einstein, 1879–1955

"I have yet to find the man, however exalted his station, who did not do better work and put forth greater effort under a spirit of approval than under a spirit of criticism."

Charles Schwab, 1937–

"Sometimes our light goes out but is rekindled into a flame by another human being. Each of us owes deepest thanks to those who have rekindled this light."

Albert Schweitzer, 1875–1965

"Feeling gratitude and not expressing it is like wrapping a present and not giving it."

William Arthur Ward, 1921–1994

"You cannot do a kindness too soon, for you never know how soon it will be too late."

Ralph Waldo Emerson, 1803–1882

"You have brains in your head. You have feet in your shoes. You can steer yourself in any direction you choose. You're on your way, and you know what you know. You are the guy who'll decide where to go."

Dr. Seuss (Theodore Geisel), 1904–1991

"Be kind and merciful. Let no one ever come to you without leaving better and happier."

Mother Teresa, 1910–1997

"Be an opener of doors for those who come after you and do not try to make the universe a blind alley."

Ralph Waldo Emerson, 1803–1882

"We should be lenient in our judgment, because often the mistakes of others would have been ours had we had the opportunity to make them."

Dr. R. L. Alsaker

"Earn as much as you can. Save as much as you can. Invest as much as you can. Give as much as you can."

Rev. John Wesley, 1707–1788

"Politeness and consideration for others is like investing pennies and getting dollars back."

Thomas Sowell, 1930–

"As we express our gratitude, we must never forget that the highest appreciation is not to utter words, but to live by them."

John F. Kennedy, 1917–1963

"Plant a kernel of wheat and you reap a pint; plant a pint and you reap a bushel. Always the law works to give you back more than you give."

Anthony Norvell

"Kind words do not cost much. They never blister the tongue or lips. They make other people good natured. They also produce their own image on men's souls, and a beautiful image it is."

Blaise Pascal, 1623–1662

"Ask not what your country can do for you. Ask what you can do for your country."

John F. Kennedy, 1917–1963

"There's nothing so rewarding as to make people realize they are worthwhile in this world."

Bob Anderson

"No act of kindness, no matter how small, is ever wasted."

Aesop, 620–560 BC

CHOICES AND DECISIONS

"What you don't do can be a destructive force."

Eleanor Roosevelt, 1884–1962

We are all faced with choices and decisions throughout our lives. It starts early and it doesn't stop. Some decisions and choices are relatively unimportant but others can be life changing, such as your choice of a career, of a college, of a friend, of a mate, of a job, of a place to live— all relatively important and in some cases life-changing.

Here are a few of the many quotes in this chapter that I think tell an important story.

"Be careful about the environment you choose for it shapes you; be careful about the friends you choose for you will become like them."

W. Clement Stone, 1902–2002

"Life is the sum of your choices."

Albert Camus, 1913–1960

"Full maturity is achieved by realizing that you have choices to make."

Angela Baron McBride

Choices are always there to be made. Not making a choice is also a choice. If you are fortunate in life to make the right choices your path through life will be easier and more successful. Experience and knowledge are key to making the right choices.

If you have the time, study each option to understand the benefits and drawbacks. Remember that you have the responsibility to make good decisions. The issue of choices and decisions is more important now than ever before in history because there are more decisions to be made. The decision tools have been enhanced by new computer technology and faster communication. We know more but have more problems.

"Many receive advice, only the wise profit from it."

Cyrus the Great, 600–529 BC

Fly with the eagles not the turkeys. I have seen good friends where one moves along more quickly on a career path and, in turn, helps his friend in some way, which can be a benefit for both.

I think of choices and decisions as the road map of my life. Where am I going, why, how, when, and who is involved? What are my goals? This all will be a part of planning and flexibility will also play a key role.

Always do
right;
this will
gratify
some people
and
astonish
others.

Mark Twain, 1835–1910

It is our
choices
that show what
we truly are far
more than our
abilities.

"We are given one life, and the decision is ours whether to wait for circumstances to make up our mind, or whether to act, and in acting, to live."

Omar Nelson Bradley, 1898–1981

"What you don't do can be a destructive force."

Eleanor Roosevelt, 1884–1962

"One's philosophy is not best expressed in words; it is expressed in the choices one makes. In the long run, we shape our lives and we shape ourselves. The process never ends until we die. And, the choices we make are ultimately our own responsibility."

Eleanor Roosevelt, 1884–1962

"The true secret of giving advice is, after you have given it, to be perfectly indifferent whether it is taken or not, and never persist in trying to set people right."

Hannah Whitall Smith, 1832–1911

"In giving advice, seek to help, not please, your friend."

Solon, 638–559 BC

"Advice is what we ask for when we already know the answer but wish we didn't."

Erica Jong, 1942–

"The strongest principle of growth lies in human choice."

George Eliot, 1819–1880

"Accept that you are where you are and what you are because of your own choices and decisions."

Brian Tracy, 1944–

"Destiny is not a matter of chance, it is a matter of choice; it is not a thing to be waited for, it is a thing to be achieved."

William Jennings Bryan, 1860–1925

"It is our choices that show what we truly are far more than our abilities."

J.K. Rowling, 1965–

PLANNING

"Before everything else, getting ready is the secret of success."

Henry Ford, 1863–1947

Planning is a necessary part of life. Plans can be as simple as check lists of what you plan to do in a day or a detailed plan of what your business is expecting to do over a period of time in terms of profit and loss. These plans can be intricate and cover every detail in every area to help produce the expected results.

A look at some of the quotes in this chapter shows the fundamentally important ways that planning can guide your efforts.

"The lame man who stays on the right road outstrips the runner who takes the wrong one—the more active and swift the latter is, the farther he will go astray."
Francis Bacon, 1561–1625

Speed in the wrong direction is a big negative. If you find that you are on the wrong road, make a correction—it may not be too late.

> *"No problem can be solved until it is reduced to some simple form. The changing of a vague difficulty into a specific, concrete form is a very essential element in thinking.*
>
> John Pierpont Morgan, 1837–1913

> *"We cannot always build the future for our youth, but we can build our youth for the future."*
>
> Franklin D. Roosevelt, 1882–1945

Teach and help your children to be ready for the future. Since we don't know what the future brings, we can begin to introduce our children to some basics about the world and maybe some basic geography and local news.

Your mental energy is limited by your physical energy. How do you develop more energy of all kinds? You start by putting your body in top physical condition. Unless you do that, all your other activities won't help much—you'll be stuck with the mental and emotional energy that you have now.

Tom Hopkins

"Intellectuals solve problems, geniuses prevent them."

Albert Einstein, 1879–1955

"We all need lots of powerful long range goals to help us past the short term obstacles."

Jim Rohn, 1930–2009

"Without leaps of imagination or dreaming, we lose the excitement of possibilities. Dreaming after all, is a form of planning."

Gloria Steinem, 1934–

"Before everything else, getting ready is the secret of success."

Henry Ford, 1863–1947

"There are risks and costs to a plan of action. But they are far less than the long range risks of comfortable inaction."

John F. Kennedy, 1917–1963

"Good habits are as easy to acquire as bad ones."

Tim McCarver, 1941–

In the long run, men hit **ONLY** what they **AIM** at.

Henry David Thoreau, 1817–1862

Life
wouldn't be worth
living
if I worried about the
future
as well as the
present.

Somerset Maugham, 1874–1965

"The sovereign invigorator of the body is exercise and of all the exercises walking is the best."

Thomas Jefferson, 1743–1826

"The trouble with our times is that the future is not what it used to be."

Paul Valery, 1871–1945

"I have always thought that one man of tolerable abilities may work great changes and accomplish great affairs among mankind if he first performs a good plan, and cutting off all amusements or other employments that would divert his attention, make the execution of that same plan his sole study and business."

Benjamin Franklin, 1706–1790

"Good manners will open doors that the best education cannot."

Clarence Thomas, 1948–

"Big goals get big results. No goals get no results or somebody else's results."

Mark Victor Hansen, 1948–

"In preparation for battle, I have always found that plans were useless, but planning is indispensable."

Dwight D. Eisenhower, 1890–1969

"I have seen the future and it doesn't work."

Robert Fulford, 1932–

"Throughout history it has been the inaction of those who could have acted, the indifference of those who should have known better, the silence of the voice of justice when it mattered most that has made it possible for evil to triumph."

Haile Selassie, 1892–1975

"Half of our life is spent trying to find something to do with the time we have rushed through life trying to save."

Will Rogers, 1879–1935

"The future will be better tomorrow."

Dan Quayle, 1941–

"The future ain't what it used to be."

Yogi Berra, 1925–

All of us tend to put off living. We are all dreaming of some *magical* rose garden over the *horizon* instead of enjoying the roses that are *blooming* outside your window today.

Dale Carnegie, 1888–1955

"You cannot speak that which you do not know. You cannot share that which you do not feel. You cannot translate that which you do not have. And you cannot give that which you do not possess. To give it and to share it, and for it to be effective, you first need to have it. Good communication starts with good preparation."

Jim Rohn, 1930–2009

"The beginning of a habit is like an invisible thread, but every time we repeat the act we strengthen the strand, add to it another filament, until it becomes a great cable and binds us irrevocably to think and act."

Orison Swett Marden, 1848–1926

"Hide not your talents, they for use were made. What's a sun dial in the shade?"

Benjamin Franklin, 1706–1790

"Manners maketh the man."

William of Wykeham, 1324–1404

PERSEVERENCE

"And say my glory was I had such friends."

William Butler Yeats, 1865–1939

Perseverance is one of the most important character traits anyone can have. History shows that many people have succeeded because they persevered. They never stopped trying and finally achieved success. These words from one of our most famous and important presidents set the stage:

"Having thus chosen our course, without guile and with pure purpose, let us renew our trust in God and go forward without our fear and with manly hearts."

Abraham Lincoln, 1809–1865

"Hard work without talent is a shame, but talent without hard work is a tragedy."

Robert Half

I have seen both cases. It's a real loss to see talent wasted. If you read biographies of successful people you will see examples of hard work.

I paraphrase the definition of perseverance as a continued effort to do or achieve something despite difficulties and failure; a steady persistence in a course of action, a purpose especially in spite of difficulties, a day to day decision not to give up.

Jackie Robinson was a famous African American baseball player who was the first to play major league baseball. He carried the burden of having to perform as a star and resist the prejudice and segregation he faced daily. He was indeed a star beginning in 1947 when he was named Rookie of the year. Two years later he was voted MVP of the league. He was elected to the National Baseball Hall of Fame in 1962.

He said:

> *"We ask for nothing special. We ask only to be permitted to live as you live, and as our nation's constitution provides."*

The message that hard work and practice are always needed to be a top performer is universally true. Billy Crystal said he became an overnight success, "but it first took 20 years in show business."

Many famous and successful people attribute their career to perseverance over a long time. Thomas Edison said that his success was based on constant trial and error. He said, "Genius is one percent inspiration and ninety-nine percent perspiration." He also said, "I have never failed once, it just happened to be a two-thousand-and-one-step process."

I am extraordinarily patient, provided I get my own way in the end.

Margaret Thatcher, 1925–

"Nothing of great value in life comes easily. The things of highest value sometimes come hard. The gold that has the greatest value lies deepest in the earth, as do the diamonds."

Norman Vincent Peale, 1898–1993

"Patience and perseverance have a magical effect before which difficulties and obstacles vanish."

John Quincy Adams, 1767–1848

"Whatever you do, you need courage. Whatever course you decide upon, there is always someone to tell you that you are wrong. There are always difficulties arising that tempt you to believe your critics are right. To map out a course of action and follow it to an end requires some of the same courage that a soldier needs. Peace has its victories, but it takes brave men and women to win them."

Ralph Waldo Emerson, 1803–1882

"I can't write a book commensurate with Shakespeare but I can write a book by me."

Sir Walter Raleigh, 1552–1618

"We are always more anxious to be distinguished for a talent which we do not possess than to be praised for the fifteen which we do possess."

Mark Twain, 1835–1910

"Few men during their lifetime come anywhere near exhausting the resources dwelling within them. There are deep wells of strength that are never used."

Richard E. Byrd, 1888–1957

"Difficulties mastered are opportunities won."

Sir Winston Churchill, 1874–1965

"Most of the important things in the world have been accomplished by people who have kept on trying when there seemed to be no hope at all."

Dale Carnegie, 1888–1955

"What this power is I cannot say; all I know is that it exists and it becomes available only when a man is in that state of mind in which he knows exactly what he wants and is fully determined not to quit until he finds it."

Alexander Graham Bell, 1847–1922

"The measure of a man is the way he bears up under misfortune."

Plutarch, 46–120 AD

"Problems are good, not bad. Welcome them and become the solution. When you have solved enough problems, people will thank you."

Mark Victor Hansen, 1948–

"How poor are they who have not patience! What wound did ever heal but by degree?"

William Shakespeare, 1564–1616

"Patience serves as a protection against wrongs, as clothes do against cold. For if you put on more clothes as the cold increases, it will have no power to hurt you. So in like manner you must grow in patience when you meet great wrongs, and they will then be powerless to vex your mind."

Leonardo da Vinci, 1452–1519

"There are two cardinal sins from which all others spring: Impatience and Laziness."

Franz Kafka, 1883–1924

In the
realm of ideas
everything depends on
enthusiasm.
In the real world,
all rests on
perseverance.

Johann Wolfgang von Goethe, 1749–1832

"The difficulties, hardships and trials of life, the obstacles. . . are positive blessings. They knit the muscles more firmly, and teach self-reliance."

William Matthews, 1942–1997

"Nothing will ever be attempted if all possible objections must first be overcome."

Samuel Johnson, 1709–1784

"Practice is the price of mastery. Whatever you practice over and over again becomes a new habit of thought and performances."

Brian Tracy, 1944–

"The flower that follows the sun does so even in cloudy days."

Robert Leighton, 1611–1684

"Fortunate is the man who has developed the self-control to steer a straight course toward his objective in life, without being swayed from his purpose by either commendation or condemnation."

Napoleon Hill, 1883–1970

"A certain amount of opposition is a great help to a man. Kites rise against not with the wind."

John Neal, 1793–1876

"With ordinary talents and extraordinary perseverance, all things are attainable."

Sir Thomas Fowell Buxton, 1786–1845

"I don't wait for moods. You accomplish nothing if you do that. Your mind must know it has to get down to work."

Pearl S. Buck, 1892–1973

"The man who can drive himself further once the effort gets painful is the man who will win."

Sir Roger Bannister, 1929–

"Practice doesn't make perfect. Perfect practice makes perfect."

Vince Lombardi, 1913–1970

"It is surprising what a man can do when he has to, and how little most men do when they don't have to."

Walter Linn

I never could have
done what I have done
without
habits
of
punctuality,
order,
and
diligence,
without
determination
to concentrate myself on
one subject at a time.

Charles Dickens, 1812–1870

"I believe in the dignity of labor, whether with head or hand—that the world owes no man a living but that it owes every man an opportunity to make a living."

John D. Rockefeller, Jr., 1874–1960

"Difficulties strengthen the mind, as labor does the body."

Marcus Annaeus Seneca, 55BC–40 AD

"Patience and fortitude conquer all things."

Ralph Waldo Emerson, 1803–1882

"Troubles are often the tools by which God fashions us for better things."

Henry Ward Beecher, 1813–1887

"Hard work spotlights the character of people; some turn up their sleeves, some turn up their noses, and some don't turn up at all."

Sam Ewing, 1920–2001

"Genius is divine perseverance. Genius I cannot have, but perseverance all can have."

Woodrow T. Wilson, 1856–1924

"It has been my observation that most people get ahead during the time that others waste time."

Henry Ford, 1863–1947

"Patience has its limits; take it too far and it's cowardice."

George Jackson, 1941–1971

"Use what talents you possess; the woods would be very silent if no birds sang there except those that sang best."

Henry Van Dyke, 1852–1933

"I know of no more encouraging fact than the unquestioned ability of a man to elevate his life by conscious endeavor."

Henry David Thoreau, 1817–1862

"Most of the important things in the world have been accomplished by people who have kept on trying when there seemed to be no help at all."

Dale Carnegie, 1888–1955

"Many men owe the grandeur of their lives to their tremendous difficulties."

Charles Haddon Spurgeon, 1834–1892

Nothing in this world can take the place of persistence. Talent will not; nothing is more common than unsuccessful men with talent. Genius will not; unrewarded genius is almost a proverb. Education will not; the world is full of educated derelicts. Persistence and determination alone are **omnipotent.**

Calvin Coolidge, 1872–1933

"Those who want to succeed will find a way, those who don't will find an excuse."

Leo Aguila

"There's a difference between interest and commitment. When you are interested in doing something, you do it only when it is convenient. When you are committed to something, you accept no excuses, only results."

Kenneth Blanchard, 1939–

"Far better it is to dare mighty things, to win glorious triumphs, even though checkered by failure than to rank with those poor spirits who neither enjoy much nor suffer much, because they live in a gray twilight that knows not victory nor defeat."

Theodore Roosevelt, 1858–1919

"We must all wage an intense, lifelong battle against the constant downward pull. If we relax, the bugs and weeds of negativity will move into the garden and take away everything of value."

Jim Rohn, 1930–2009

SUCCESS

"Do what you can, with what you have, where you are."

Theodore Roosevelt, 1858–1919

Success is reaching a level of wealth or achievement considered to be the accomplishment of a goal that you set. However, it is your definition of success that is important.

We each have definitions of success that fit our personal goals and that don't necessarily include wealth. The goal could be to write a book and have it published. It could be finding and securing the right job or mate. Here are a couple of quotes that give it more meaning.

> *"If money is your hope for independence you will never have it. The only real security that a man will have in this world is a reserve of knowledge, experience, and ability."*
>
> Henry Ford, 1863–1947

In today's world this is especially true. What do you know and how valuable is it to a potential employer? The message is, learn and continue to learn until you are someday a valuable employee.

> *"Doing what you love to do is the cornerstone of having abundance in your life."*
>
> Wayne Dyer, 1940–

This has been said in many different ways but it is a foundation for success and happiness. You could find something you love to do and then make a living doing it. Or you could do what you love aside from what you do for a living.

> *"I find my greatest pleasure, and so my reward, in the work that precedes what the world calls success."*
>
> Thomas Edison, 1887-1931

A lot of hard work goes into any success. You can't and shouldn't forget the small victories and defeats along the way.

Failure

is

the

opportunity

to begin again,

more

intelligently.

Henry Ford, 1863-1947

"Success is the ability to go from one failure to another with no loss of enthusiasm."

Sir Winston Churchill, 1874–1965

"Let us be thankful for the fools. But for them, the rest of us could not succeed."

Mark Twain, 1835–1910

"Carpe diem! Rejoice while you are alive; enjoy the day; live life to the fullest; make the most of what you have. It is later than you think."

Horace, 65–8 BC

"If a man has talent and cannot use it, he has failed. If he has a talent and uses only half of it, he has partly failed. If he has talent and learns somehow to use the whole of it, he has gloriously succeeded and has a satisfaction and a triumph few men ever know."

Thomas Wolfe, 1900–1938

"There is always room for those who can be relied on to deliver the goods when they say they will."

Napoleon Hill, 1883–1970

"Formulate and stamp indelibly in your mind a mental picture of yourself succeeding. Hold this picture tenaciously. Never permit it to fade. Your mind will seek to develop the picture."

Norman Vincent Peale, 1898–1993

"The Chinese use two brush strokes to write the word "crisis." One brush stroke stands for danger, the other for opportunity. In a crisis, be aware of danger but recognize the opportunity."

John F. Kennedy, 1917–1963

"Shallow men believe in luck, wise and strong men in cause and effect."

Ralph Waldo Emerson, 1803–1882

"A winner is someone who recognized his God given talent, works his tail off to develop them into skills, and uses these skills to accomplish his goals."

Larry Bird, 1956–

"I not only use all the brains I have but all I can borrow."

Woodrow T. Wilson, 1856–1924

Only those who dare to *fail greatly* can ever *achieve greatly.*

John F. Kennedy, 1917–1963

"Only those who will risk going too far can possibly find out how far they can go."

T.S. Eliot, 1888–1965

"Read an hour every day in your chosen field. This works out to about one book per week, 50 books per year, and will guarantee your success."

Brian Tracy, 1944–

"For true success, ask yourself these four questions: Why? Why not? Why not me? Why not now?"

James Allen, 1864–1912

"Take a chance! All life is a chance. The man who goes the furthest is generally the one who is willing to do and dare. The 'sure thing' boat never gets far from shore."

Dale Carnegie, 1888–1955

"A man, as a general rule, owes very little to what he was born with; a man is what he makes of himself."

Alexander Graham Bell, 1847–1922

Somehow I can't believe that there are any heights that can't be scaled by a man who knows the secrets of making dreams come true. This special secret, it seems to me, can be summarized in four C's. They are

**Curiosity,
Confidence,
Courage,**
and
Courage,

and
Constancy

and the greatest of all is

Confidence.

When you believe in a thing, believe in it all the way, implicitly and unquestionably.

Walt Disney, 1901–1966

"Do not blame anybody for your mistakes and failures."

Bernard M. Baruch, 1870–1965

"The greatest thing a man can do in this world is to make the most possible out of the stuff that has been given to him. This is success, and there is no other."

Orison Swett Marden, 1848–1926

"You can succeed if no one else believes it, but you will never succeed if you don't believe in yourself."

William Boetcker, 1873–1962

"The more you seek security the less you have. But the more you seek opportunity, the more likely it is you will achieve the security that you desire."

Brian Tracy, 1944–

"Many of life's failures are people who did not realize how close they were to success when they gave up."

Thomas A. Edison, 1847–1931

"We all have a few failures under our belt. It's what makes us ready for the successes."

Randy K. Milholland

"Often the difference between a successful man and a failure is not one's better abilities or ideas, but the courage that one has to bet on his ideas, to take a calculated risk—and to act."

Maxwell Maltz, 1899–1995

"The secret of success in life is for a man to be ready for his opportunity when it comes."

Benjamin Disraeli, 1804–1881

"Opportunities multiply when they are seized; die when they are neglected. Life is a long line of opportunities."

John Wicker

"No one lives long enough to learn everything they need to learn starting from scratch. To be successful, we absolutely, positively have to find people who have already paid the price to learn the things that we need to achieve our goals."

Brian Tracy, 1944–

A minute's success pays the failures of years.

Robert Browning, 1812–1889

"Do what you can, with what you have, where you are."

Theodore Roosevelt, 1858–1919

"There is a master key to success, with which no man can fail. It is simplicity, reducing to the simplest possible terms every problem."

Henri Deterding, 1866–1939

"If you want to be truly successful, invest in yourself to get the knowledge you need to find your unique factor. When you find it, focus on it and persevere. Your success will blossom."

Giacomo Leopardi, 1798–1837

"The ideas I stand for are not mine. I borrowed them from Socrates. I swiped them from Lord Chesterfield. I stole them from Jesus. And I put them in a book. If you don't like their rules, whose do you use?"

Dale Carnegie, 1888–1955

"You'll miss 100% of the shots you don't take."

Wayne Gretzky, 1961–

CHARACTER

"You cannot be lonely if you like the person you're alone with."

Wayne Dyer, 1940–

Defined as the sum of one's traits and habits, character is the essence of who you are. How would you describe yourself? What is strong? What is weak?

The Josephson Institute defines the six pillars of character as: Trustworthiness, Respect, Responsibility, Fairness, Caring, and Citizenship.

The quotes about character that mostly impact me are:

> *"Any fool can criticize and condemn and most fools do. But it takes character and self-control to be understanding and forgiving."*
>
> Dale Carnegie, 1888–1955

> *"Character cannot be developed in ease and quiet. Only through trial and suffering can a soul be strengthened, ambition inspired, and success achieved."*
>
> Helen Keller, 1880–1968

Helen Keller was deaf and blind and yet was able to make many contributions as a speaker, writer, and a symbol of what one can achieve with enormous handicaps.

> *"The best index to a person's character is: a) how he treats people who can't do him any good, and b) how he treats people who can't fight back."*
>
> Abigail Van Buren, 1918—

Have you ever seen the complete distain and disregard by people for others who can be of no help to them? There are many indicators of a person's character and this is one of them.

Own more than thou showest,
speak less than thou knowest.

William Shakespeare, 1564–1616

"You cannot be lonely if you like the person you're alone with."

Wayne Dyer, 1940–

"You can tell the character of every man when you see how he receives praise."

Seneca, 5 BC–65 AD

"Personality can open doors, but only character can keep them open."

Elmer G. Letterman

"Character isn't something you were born with and can't change, like your fingerprints. It's something you weren't born with and must take responsibility for forming."

Jim Rohn, 1930–2009

"One man practicing sportsmanship is far better than a hundred teaching it."

Knute Rockne, 1888–1931

"Why is it that people who cannot show feelings presume that is a strength and not a weakness?"

Max Sarton

"Be more concerned with your character than your reputation. Your character is what you really are while your reputation is merely what others think you are."

John Wooden, 1910–2010

"Lord Bacon told Sir Edward Coke when he was boasting, the less you speak of your greatness, the more shall I think of it."

William Shakespeare, 1564–1616

FLEXIBILITY

"The true sign of intelligence is not knowledge but imagination."

Albert Einstein, 1879–1955

We must be prepared to meet the uncertainties of life. Change comes and we must be flexible. Being flexible enough to adjust or change our direction is a necessary part of life. Change is now more prevalent than ever with computers, new technologies, communication, and the speed of change affecting everything.

Some quotes that come to mind and are important:

> *"To improve is to change; to be perfect is to change often."*
>
> Sir Winston Churchill, 1874–1965

Change breeds flexibility and results in new methods.

"When one door closes another opens, but we often look so long and so regretfully upon the closed door that we do not see the ones which open for us."

Alexander Graham Bell, 1847–1922

We do not live an equal life, but one of contrast and patchwork; now a little joy, then a sorrow, now a sin, then a generous or brave action.

Ralph Waldo Emerson, 1803–1882

"When you focus on what might have been, it gets in the way of what can be."

Patricia Fripp

"The best way to have a good idea is to have lots of ideas."

Linus Pauling, 1902–1994

"The true sign of intelligence is not knowledge but imagination."

Albert Einstein, 1879–1955

"Sunshine is delicious, rain is refreshing, wind braces us up, snow is exhilarating; there is really no such thing as bad weather, only different kinds of weather."

John Ruskin, 1819–1900

"One of the virtues of being very young is that you don't let the facts get in the way of your imagination."

Sam Levenson, 1911–1980

"We are always eighteen months away from failure."

Bill Gates, 1955–

Some men see things as they are and say,

WHY?

I dream of things that never were and say,

WHY NOT?

George Bernard Shaw, 1856–1950

"There are two primary choices in life: to accept conditions as they exist, or accept the responsibility for changing them."

Denis Waitley, 1933–

"The surest way to corrupt a youth is to instruct him to hold in higher esteem those who think alike than those who think differently."

Friedrich Nietzsche, 1844–1900

"The only man I know who behaves sensibly is my tailor: he takes my measurements anew each time he sees me. The rest go on with their old measurements and expect me to fit them."

George Bernard Shaw, 1865–1950

"Everyone thinks of changing the world, but no one thinks of changing himself."

Count Leo Tolstoy, 1828–1910

"Whenever there is a hard job to be done I assign it to a lazy man; he is sure to find an easy way of doing it."

Walter Chrysler, 1875–1940

LEARNING

*"If you thoroughly know anything, teach it
to others."*

Tyron Edwards, 1809–1894

Learning is the basis for all progress from the beginning of time. It certainty is the foundation of all the chapters in this book. No subject could be presented and discussed without something learned first as a base.

The quotes in this chapter cover many aspects of learning and teaching from ancient times to the present.

> *"Never seem more learned than the people you are
> with. Wear your learning like a pocket watch and keep
> it hidden. Do not pull it out to count the hours but give
> the time when you are asked."*
>
> Lord Chesterfield, 1694–1773

This is a profound statement from a true statesman. Don't be a "know-it-all" or have an answer for everyone on everything—only when it is appropriate, pull out your answers.

> *"To repeat what others have said requires education; to challenge it requires brains."*
>
> Mary Pettibone

It's easy to repeat and agree but that's not always the right action. When you have a different opinion and need to discuss it, be prepared to support your position.

A strong interest in reading is a big advantage for young people and should be encouraged. Larry King, the TV talk show host said, "I remind myself every morning, nothing I say this day will teach me anything, so if I'm going to learn, I must do it by listening."

> *"Much learning does not teach understanding."*
>
> Heraclitus, 540–480 BC, Greek philosopher

There is a distinct difference between the accumulation of knowledge and the proper use of it. Understanding is a combination of many things including common sense and experience.

Learning is the key to civilization. Without good teachers, students willing to learn, and support from those who realize its importance to our future, learning will stagnate.

I cannot teach anyone anything. I can only make them think.

Socrates, 469–399

To
know
that we
know
what we
know
and that we do not
know
what we do not
KNOW,
this is true knowledge.

Henry Thoreau, 1817–1862

"Learning is not compulsory. . . Neither is survival."

W. Edward Deming, 1900–1993

"Whoever ceases to be a student has never been a student."

George Hess

"Whoever neglects learning in his youth loses the past and is dead for the future."

Euripides, 484–406 BC

"Learning is not attained by chance, it must be sought for with ardor and attended to with diligence."

Abigail Adams, 1744–1818

"If you are not moving closer to what you want in sales (or in your life) you probably aren't doing enough asking."

Jack Canfield, 1944–

"If you have knowledge, let others light their candles with it."

Sir Winston Churchill, 1874–1965

"The wisest mind has something yet to learn."

George Santayana, 1863–1952

"If you are interested, you never have to look for new interests. They come to you. When you are genuinely interested in one thing, it will always lead to something else."

Eleanor Roosevelt, 1884–1962

"Millions saw the apple fall, but Newton was the one who asked `why?'"

Bernard Baruch, 1870–1965

"If you thoroughly know anything, teach it to others."

Tyron Edwards, 1809–1894

"For the things we have to learn before we can do them, we learn by doing them."

Aristotle, 384–322 BC

"Whenever you are asked if you can do a job, tell them, 'Certainly I can!' Then get busy and find out how to do it."

Theodore Roosevelt, 1858–1919

We learn
by
example
and by
direct experience
because there are
real limits
to the adequacy
of
verbal instructions.

Malcolm Gladwell, 1963–

A major stimulant to
creative thinking
is
focused questions.
There is something about a
well-worded
question
that often penetrates to the
heart of the matter
and triggers
new ideas
and
INSIGHTS.

Brian Tracy, 1944–

"A prudent man should always follow in the path trodden by great men and imitate those who are most excellent."

Niccolo Machiavelli, 1469–1527

"The great aim of education is not knowledge but action."

Herbert Spencer, 1820–1903

"Anyone who stops learning is old, whether at 20 or 80. Anyone who keeps learning stays young. The greatest thing in life is to keep your mind young."

Henry Ford, 1863–1947

"A wise man when asked how he learned so much about everything, replied: By never being ashamed or afraid to ask questions about anything of which I am ignorant."

John Abbott, 1821–1893

"What we want is to see the child in pursuit of knowledge, not knowledge in pursuit of the child."

George Bernard Shaw, 1856–1950

"Next in importance to freedom and justice is popular education without which neither freedom nor justice can be permanently maintained."

James A. Garfield, 1831–1881

"It is the mark of an educated mind to be able to entertain a thought without accepting it."

Aristotle, 384–322 BC

"An education isn't how much you have committed to memory, or even how much you know. It's being able to differentiate between what you do know and what you don't."

Anatole France, 1844–1924

"Perhaps the most valuable result of all education is the ability to make yourself do the thing you have to do, when it ought to be done, whether you like it or not; it is the first lesson that ought to be learned; and however early a man's training begins, it is probably the last lesson that he learns thoroughly."

Thomas H. Huxley, 1825–1895

"Judge a man by his questions rather than by his answers."

Voltaire, 1694–1778

"Fathers send their sons to college either because they went to college or because they didn't."

L.L. Henderson, 1888–1957

WISDOM AND
JUDGMENT

"In youth we learn; in age we understand."

Marie Eschenbach, 1830–1916

Wisdom is a prized asset that we all want. It is defined in several dictionaries as a deep understanding and realization of people, things, events, or situations—the quality or state of being wise, knowledge coupled with what is right and just. It is the ability to discern inner qualities. Finally, it can be difficult to define but people generally recognize it when they encounter it.

Judgement is the evaluation of evidence or information to make a decision. It is often related to legal issues, but not limited to that.

Here are some great quotes:

"There are essentially two things that will make us wiser, the books that we read and the people we meet."
Charles "Tremendous" Jones

It's hard to deny this quote. Think about how we learn and get wiser. The power of books and people, the right people who can teach you something, will make the difference. You can read a book a week, if you read an hour each night. That's over fifty books a year on a disciplined basis.

"Never trust the advice of a man in difficulties."
Aesop, 620–560 BC

The man in difficulties may not be a good advisor for two reasons—his problems could have been caused by poor judgment or he may be trying to use you to get out of his bad situation. Seek a better source of advice; someone with a history of success.

Wisdom

doesn't necessarily come with

age.

Sometimes

age

just shows up all by itself.

Woodrow Wilson, 1856–1924

Wisdom

doesn't automatically come with old age. Nothing does except

wrinkles.

It's true, some wines improve with age, but only if the grapes are good in the first place.

Abigail Van Buren, 1918—

"We judge ourselves by what we feel capable of doing, while others judge us by what we have done."

Henry Wadsworth Longfellow, 1807–1882

"In youth we learn; in age we understand."

Marie Eschenbach, 1830–1916

"To acquire knowledge, one must study: but to acquire wisdom, one must observe."

Marilyn vos Savant, 1946–

"You must constantly ask yourself these questions: Who am I around? What are they doing to me? What have they got me reading? What have they got me saying? Where do they have me going? What do they have me thinking? And most important, what do they have me becoming? Then ask yourself the big question: Is that okay? "

Jim Rohn, 1930–2009

"Experience is not what happens to a man; it is what a man does with what happens to him."

Aldous Huxley, 1894–1963

"Understanding can overcome any situation, however mysterious or insurmountable it may appear to be."

Norman Vincent Peale, 1898–1993

"But as I look back at my life, it is easy to see that the times when my wisdom and understanding grew to new levels; those times when I approached becoming the person I long to be; it was always the times that followed negative circumstances."

Vic Johnson

"In a heated argument we are apt to lose sight of the truth."

Publilius Syrus, 100 BC

"Good people are good because they've come to wisdom through failure."

William Saroyan, 1908–1981

"The whole problem with the world is that fools and fanatics are always so certain of themselves, but wiser people so full of doubt."

Bertram Russell, 1872–1970

Rule no.1:
Use your own
good judgment
in all situations.
There will be no
additional rules.

John Nordstrom, 1871–1963

"True wisdom comes to each of us when we realize how little we understand ourselves and the world around us."

Socrates, 469–399 BC

"Experience teaches only the teachable."

Aldous Huxley, 1894–1963

"The older I grow the more I distrust the familiar doctrine that age brings wisdom."

H. L. Mencken, 1880–1956

COMMUNICATION

"A person hears only what they understand."

Johann Wolfgang von Goethe, 1794–1832

The way we connect in life is communication, whether it be by voice, computer, telephone, or some other way.

"Poor or fuzzy communication are major time wasters. Take the time to be crystal clear in your communication with others."

Brian Tracy, 1944–

Communicating is one of the most important functions in business or life. If the information being given by you isn't totally true and accurate, then there will be a problem. Think of the times when someone inadvertently gave you incorrect instruction or directions and the problems it caused you.

"The less you talk, the more you are listened to."
Abigail VanBuren, 1910–2002

Listening is a skill you must develop. You can hear but not listen. Learn how to concentrate and process information from people who have important information. When you talk make it worth the listener's time. Develop a reputation for being one who has valuable information and not one who frequently talks but has little of value to say.

Nature has given us
two ears,
two eyes
and
one tongue
to the end that we should
hear
and

see

more than we
speak.

Socrates, 469–399 BC

"A person hears only what they understand."

Johann Wolfgang von Goethe, 1794–1832

"Silence is never more golden than when you hold it long enough to get all the facts before you speak."

Unknown author

"The difference between the right word and the almost right word is the difference between lightning and the lightning bug."

Mark Twain, 1835–1910

"Are you really listening. . . or are you just waiting your turn to talk?"

Robert Montgomery, 1807–1855

"Your very silence shows you agree."

Euripides, 484– 406 BC

"He who strikes the first blow admits he's lost the argument."

Chinese Proverb

"Seek first to understand and then to be understood."

Stephen R. Covey, 1932–2012

LEADERSHIP AND GOVERNMENT

"Anyone can hold the helm when the sea is calm."

Publilius Syrus, 100 BC

This is a subject of importance to everyone, not only now but for the future. Good government is a blessing but history shows that many cities and countries have never had good leadership and government. This is a top priority and should be expected by all citizens.

Here is a sampling of quotes about leadership and government.

> *"Power is no blessing in itself, except when it is used to protect the innocent."*
>
> Jonathon Swift, 1667–1745

"Management is efficiency in climbing the corporate ladder of success; leadership determines whether the ladder is leaning against the right wall."

Steven R. Covey, 1932–2012

This is a good comparison between management and leadership. Leadership comes first and sets the direction.

Leadership

is not magnetic personality—
that can just as well be a
glib tongue.
It is not making friends
and influencing people—
that is flattery.
Leadership is lifting a
person's vision to higher levels,
the raising of a person's
performance to a higher
standard, the building of
a personality
beyond normal limits.

Peter Drucker, 1909–2005

"One of the hardest tasks of leadership is understanding that you are not what you are but what you're perceived to be by others."

Edward L. Flom

"There is only one boss: the customer. And he can fire everybody in the company, from the chairman on down, simply by spending his money somewhere else."

Sam Walton, 1918–1992

"Anyone can hold the helm when the sea is calm."

Publilius Syrus, 100 BC

"When you step into a turnaround situation, you can safely assume four things: morale is low, fear is high, the good people are halfway out the door, and the slackers are hiding."

Nina Disesa

"There is only one way to get anybody to do anything and that is by making the other person want to do it."

Dale Carnegie, 1888–1955

Leadership
is simply an
energy
that mobilizes
people
and moves
them.

Doug Firebaugh

Leadership
appears to be the art
of
getting others to want
to do
something
you are convinced
should
be done.

Vance Packard, 1914–1997

"In general, the art of government consists of taking as much money as possible from one party of the citizens to give to the other."

Voltaire, 1694–1778

"Six traits of effective leaders: 1. Make others feel important, 2. Promote a vision, 3. Follow the golden rule, 4. Admit mistakes, 5. Criticize others only in private, 6. Stay close to the action, example has more followers than reason. We unconsciously imitate what pleases us, and approximate to the characters we most admire."

John Christian Bovee, 1820–1904

"I contend for a nation to try to tax itself into prosperity is like a man standing in a bucket and trying to lift himself up by the handle."

Sir Winston Churchill, 1874–1965

"Hire the best, pay them fairly, communicate frequently, provide challenges and rewards and believe in them. Get out of their way and they'll knock your socks off."

Mary Ann Allison

"Pull the string and it will follow wherever you wish. Push it, and it will go nowhere at all."

Dwight D. Eisenhower, 1890–1969

"Leadership is practiced not so much in words as in attitude and in actions."

Harold S. Geneen, 1910–1997

"Nothing is so strong as gentleness and nothing is so gentle as real strength."

Ralph W. Sockman, 1889–1970

"In order to be a leader, a man must have followers. And to have followers, a man must have their confidence. Hence, the supreme quality for a leader is unquestionably integrity. Without it, no real success is possible, no matter whether it is on a section gang, a football field, in an army, or as in an office. If a man's associations find him guilty of being phony, if they find that he lacks forthright integrity, he will fail. His teachings and actions must square with each other. The first great need, therefore, is integrity and high purpose."

Dwight D. Eisenhower, 1890–1969

If your actions
inspire
others to
dream more,
learn more,
do more,
and
become more,
you are a
leader.

John Quincy Adams, 1767–1848

"Giving money and power to government is like giving whiskey and car keys to teenage boys."

P. J. O'Rourke, 1947–

"A government which robs Peter to pay Paul can always depend on the support of Paul."

George Bernard Shaw, 1856–1950

"The only difference between a tax man and a taxidermist is that the taxidermist leaves the skin."

Mark Twain, 1835–1910

"There is no distinctly native American criminal class—save Congress."

Mark Twain, 1835–1910

"A government big enough to give you everything you want, is strong enough to take everything you have."

Thomas Jefferson, 1743–1826

"Flexibility in a time of great change is a vital quality of leadership."

Brian Tracy, 1944–

TRUTH, TRUST, AND FREEDOM

"If it is not right do not do it; if it is not true do not say it."

Marcus Aurelius, 121–180 AD

We all seek the truth because it's the only way we can make correct decisions. Whether the choice you have to make is minor or major, you need the truth, the facts. If you are receiving incorrect information you will likely make the wrong decision.

Trust is an assured reliance on the character, ability, strength, or truth of someone or something.

Truth and trust are natural partners. If you have the truth, people will trust you; if people trust you it's because you tell the truth.

You can see that truth and trust exist in an atmosphere of freedom. A government that has truth and trust will also have freedom.

Some revealing quotes are written here.

> *"Facts do not cease to exist because they are ignored."*
> Aldous Huxley, 1894–1963

> *"The man who fears no truth has nothing to fear from lies."*
> Thomas Jefferson, 1743–1826

> *"If you tell the truth you don't have to remember anything."*
> Mark Twain, 1835–1910

Think of the complications that lies create, think of the consequences and how much better and easier it is to be truthful. Sir Walter Scott, Scottish novelist and poet, said, "Oh what a tangled web we weave, when first we practice to deceive."

If it is not right
DO NOT DO IT;

if it is not true
DO NOT SAY IT.

Marcus Aurelius, 121–180 AD

Truth is a thing **immortal** and **perpetual,** and it gives to us the **beauty** that fades not away in **time.**

Frank Norris, 1870–1902

"A man who doesn't trust himself can never truly trust anyone else."

Cardinal de Retz, 1613–1679

"Do not trust all men but trust men of worth; the former course is silly, the latter a mark of prudence."

Democritus, 460 BC–370 BC

"The chief lesson I have learned in a long life is that the only way to make a man trustworthy is to trust him, and the surest way to make him untrustworthy is to distrust him and show your distrust."

Henry L. Stimson, 1867–1950

"Integrity is telling myself the truth. And honesty is telling the truth to other people."

Spencer Johnson

"Whenever you are to do a thing, though it can never be known but to yourself, ask yourself how would you act were all the world looking at you, and act accordingly."

Thomas Jefferson, 1743–1826

"For it is mutual trust, even more than mutual interest that holds human associations together. Our friends seldom profit us but they make us feel safe. Marriage is a scheme to accomplish exactly that same end."

H.L. Mencken, 1880–1956

"Truth will always be truth, regardless of lack of understanding, disbelief, or ignorance."

W. Clement Stone, 1902–2002

"I am not bound to win, but I am bound to be true. I am not bound to succeed but I am bound to live the best life that I can have. I must stand with anybody that stands right and part from him when he does wrong."

Abraham Lincoln, 1809–1865

"Dishonesty is like a boomerang. About the time you think all is well, it hits you in the back of the head."

Unknown author

"A liar should have a good memory."

Quintilian, 35–100 AD

"I never gave anybody hell. I just told the truth and they thought it was hell."

Harry S. Truman, 1884–1972

"They that give up essential liberty to obtain a little temporary safety deserve neither liberty nor safety."

Benjamin Franklin, 1706–1790

"In the truest sense, freedom cannot be bestowed; it must be achieved."

Franklin D. Roosevelt, 1882–1945

"Truth is a thing immortal and perpetual, and it gives to us the beauty that fades not away in time."

Frank Norris, 1870–1902

Freedom

has its life in the hearts, the actions, the spirit of men and so it must be daily earned and refreshed

else like a flower cut from its life giving roots, it will wither and die.

Dwight D. Eisenhower, 1890–1969

BIOGRAPHIES

John Abbott, 1821–1893, Canadian politician

Abigail Adams, 1744–1818

Abigail Adams, wife of President John Adams, understood the effort to learn. One of her children, John Quincy, became our 6th president. She was considered a strong and helpful influence on her husband during their 54 years of marriage. She was the stable influence and a strong advocate for women's rights. There is a fascinating record of their lives and times described in thousands of letters written between them.

John Quincy Adams, 1767–1848, 6th President of United States of America

Son of John Adams, the 2nd president, John Quincy served in many diplomatic roles. He was also a governor, congressman, Vice President and finally President. He was elected president in a very close race against Andrew Jackson but he lost to Jackson in the next election. It is generally acknowledged that not much was accomplished in his first and only term. It was to his credit that he was anti-slavery at a time when many were pro-slavery.

Aesop, 620–560 BC, Greek author and philosopher

Aesop was known for his fables. They were simple stories to illustrate moral lessons. Erasmus published an edition of his fables in Latin in 1513 which was widely used in schools. They are still in print and available to read today.

Leo Aguila

Muhammad Ali, 1942–, American boxing champion and sports celebrity

Ali was formerly Cassius Clay before joining the Black Muslims in 1964. His boxing career was highly successful, starting as the Olympic champion in 1960 and then winning the world heavy weight championship in 1964. He had some problems with the United States government that were overturned in his favor in 1967. He restarted his career and achieved success again. He retired in 1981 and was diagnosed with Parkinson's disease in 1996. He became a spokesman for the disease and remains a world-wide celebrity, wherever he goes.

James Allen, 1864–1912, British author and speaker

Mary Ann Allison, writer

Dr. R. L. Alsaker, American medical doctor and author

St. Ambrose, 339–397, Italian bishop and writer

Bob Anderson

Aristotle, 384–322 BC, Greek philosopher and scientist

Aristotle was an influential and important figure in the history of Western thought. He went to Athens to study under Plato and then became a teacher there. He was appointed to teach the son of King Philip II who was thirteen at the time and later became known as Alexander the Great. Aristotle's writings covered vast fields of knowledge. His work exerted an enormous influence on medieval philosophy and the whole western intellectual and scientific tradition.

Heather Armstrong, 1975–, American author and blogger

W.H. Auden, 1907–1973, American poet and essayist

Marcus Aurelius, 121–180 AD, Roman Emperor and philosopher

Marcus Aurelius had a complicated youth but he succeeded to the throne and spent most of his life fighting wars and settling disputes in the huge Roman Empire. By all reports, he was a fair and sensitive ruler considered by his people to be a role model of the perfect emperor. He wrote 12 books of his meditations that survived and have benefited history. He died shortly after a final victory. He was succeeded by his son, Commodus, and this was the beginning of a long line of bad rule and decline.

Francis Bacon, 1561–1626, English philosopher and statesman

Francis Bacon, 1909–1992, artist

Bacon was a prolific artist and a technical perfectionist. He destroyed much of his own work because it didn't meet his standards. His works, however, are in many of the major collections and he is considered to be the most important British postwar artist.

Sir Roger Bannister, 1929–, British runner

Bannister was an accomplished runner in college and became the first to break the 4 minute barrier (3 min 59.4 seconds) for the mile in 1954. After this he had a distinguished medical career and was knighted in 1975. He knew the effort needed to achieve this extraordinary feat.

Dave Barry, 1947–, American humorist, novelist and columnist

Bernard M. Baruch, 1870–1965, American statesman and financier

Baruch made his fortune on Wall Street before the depression in 1929 that severely damaged the country. He was a political advisor to President Franklin Roosevelt and to Winston Churchill during World War II and served on many important commissions.

Henry Ward Beecher, 1813–1887, American clergyman and author

Henry Beecher was an early antislavery advocate who supported the Civil War, organizing a regiment from his church for the war effort. When the war was over, he supported reconciliation rather than punishment and severe penalties on the Confederacy.

Alexander Graham Bell, 1847–1922, Scottish born American, inventor of the telephone

Bell was born in Scotland, lived in London and moved to Boston where he was a teacher for the deaf. He invented the telephone and founded the Bell telephone company. He had many difficult years of trial and error while inventing the telephone. He knew the value of perseverance.

Yogi Berra, 1925–, American Hall of Fame baseball player for the New York Yankees

Yogi Berra was a great natural baseball player and one of the best of all time. He set numerous records including playing in 14 world series and the most home runs hit by a catcher. He also managed the New York Yankees, the New York Mets, and the Houston Astros. He is famous for his use of the English language and he said some of the funniest things without ever intending that they would be funny. His most famous quote was, "It ain't over till it's over."

Larry Bird, 1956–, American professional basketball player and Hall of Fame honoree

Kenneth Blanchard, 1939–, American author, speaker and teacher

Blanchard was the co- author of *The One Minute Manager*,

a book that sold millions of copies. He has also written other books and is a frequent speaker. His co-author for *The One Minute Manager* was Spencer Johnson, a medical doctor and author of the best-selling book, *Who Moved my Cheese*.

William Boetcker, 1873–1962, American church leader and speaker

Edward De Bono, 1933–, Maltese author and consultant

John Christian Bovee, 1820–1904, American author, lawyer

Omar Nelson Bradley, 1898–1981, American general and Chairman of Joint Chiefs of Staff

Bradley was a famous general in World War II and, with Dwight Eisenhower, led the United States of America to a vital victory, winning the war. He knew how events, choices and decisions can radically change your life. He had to make decisions that affected the lives of thousands of our soldiers.

Robert Browning, 1812–1889, English poet

Anatole Broyard, 1920–1990, literary critic

William Jennings Bryan, 1860–1925, American politician and trial lawyer

Bryan served in the congress and ran unsuccessfully three times for the presidency. He was known as a skilled orator and was a trial lawyer. He was also known for his support for the common man and as a pacifist. He had a famous trial where he assisted the prosecutor against a teacher named John Scopes, who was teaching evolution in school. It became known as the *Scopes Monkey Trial*.

Pearl S. Buck, 1892–1973, American novelist and Nobel Prize winner

Pearl S. Buck was the daughter of missionaries and spent her early years in China but was educated in the U.S.A. She eventually returned to China to teach. Her first successful novel, *The Good Earth*, was about China and was a runaway best seller. She wrote other well-known novels about China and won the Nobel Prize for Literature in 1938. Several of her books became successful movies.

George Louis Leclerc Buffon, 1707–1788, French naturalist

George Burns, 1896–1996, American comedian and actor

George Burns was a very popular and successful performer who saw success for about 90 years. He started as a child actor and died at age of 100, performing almost to the end. He was accepted by every generation. He even won an Academy Award for acting in 1975 at the age of 79.

Sir Thomas Fowell Buxton, 1786–1845, English social reformer

The author Thomas Buxton was in favor of prison reform and the abolition of slavery. His efforts were part of eventual reforms. He was also head of an anti-slavery party.

Richard E. Byrd, 1888–1957, American U.S. Naval officer and explorer

As a naval officer he explored the Antarctic. With his friend, the pilot Floyd Bennett, he claimed to have made the first flight over the North Pole and they were awarded the Congressional Medal of Honor that year, 1929. In that same year he flew over the South Pole, Antarctica, and established a base for further expeditions. He was truly a pioneer and knew the strength needed to survive.

Albert Camus, 1913–1960, French author and Nobel Prize winner for literature

Jack Canfield, 1944–, best-selling author of Chicken Soup for the Soul

Dale Carnegie, 1888–1955, American author, speaker, and teacher

Carnegie was a pioneer in public speaking and personality development. His bestseller *How to Win Friends and Influence People*, a book that sold over 10 million copies, is still in print today, and has been translated into over 30 languages. He was one of the first to introduce self-improvement skills and teaching. He also started The Dale Carnegie Institute for Effective Speaking and Human Relations, which still exists and enrolls thousands of students yearly. He was proof of his own words, that success is the result of persistence, patience, and initiative.

Dick Cavett, 1936–, American comedian and TV host

Lord Chesterfield, 1694–1773, British statesman

Walter Chrysler, 1875–1940, Chrysler Corporation founder

Jill Churchill, American author

Sir Winston Churchill, 1874–1965, British Prime Minister, artist, author, and Nobel Prize winner

Churchill was in so many ways a remarkable man. He will be remembered for his leadership of Britain during the Second World War. He spent time and effort prior to the war trying to convince President Roosevelt of the United States of America to help England to prepare for this large war. He could see it coming when few of his countrymen agreed with him. He knew what it was to try and fail and do it again until success finally came. He won the Nobel Prize for Literature along with numerous other awards. When he died in 1965, 20 years after the war, there were thousands of people lining the streets and visiting the church where his body lay. He was a symbol of freedom and victory to the free world.

Marcus Tullius Cicero, 106–43 BC, Roman orator, statesman

A Roman philosopher, orator, statesman, and lawyer, he was from a wealthy family. He was considered one of Rome's greatest orators. He introduced Romans to Greek philosophy. His lost letters, discovered by Petrarch, were credited for influencing the 14th century Renaissance. He is said to have had an impact on John Locke in the 18th century. His works rank among the most influential in European culture, even today. He believed his political career was his most important achievement. Following Caesar's death he became an enemy of Mark Antony. As a consequence, Cicero was considered an enemy of the state and was murdered in 43 BC.

Calvin Coolidge, 1872–1933, 30th President of USA

He could see the true value of persistence and realized that it made the difference between success and failure. It's easy to give up and go on to something else, but you could be sacrificing the chance for a great victory. Coolidge was Vice President to Warren Harding, who died in office, and so became president in 1920. He was reelected in 1924 but did not run for a second term. He was successful with policies favorable to business and introduced the policy of sending surplus food overseas to increase farm income.

Bill Cosby, 1937–, American comedian and actor

Stephen R. Covey, 1932–2012, American author, speaker, educator, and consultant

His book, *The Seven Habits of Highly Effective People*, has sold more than 25 million copies in multiple languages. He was a graduate of Univ. of Utah, Harvard Graduate Business School, and Brigham Young University with a PhD. He built a successful consulting company and was recognized as a top management expert. He was listed as one of *Time Magazine*'s 25 most influential Americans. He believed that every person can control their destiny with proper guidance. He also wrote, *The Seven Habits of Highly Effective Families*. He was co-founder and vice chairman of Franklin Covey, a leading global professional services firm with offices in 123 countries.

Cyrus the Great, 580–521 BC founder of Persian Empire

He was the first emperor of Persia who issued a decree on his aims and policies. This was the first charter of rights, known as the first declaration of human rights. He ruled over a multi-cultured group of people from different backgrounds that co-existed in peace.

Clarence Darrow, 1857–1938, American defense attorney

W. Edward Deming, 1900–1993, American business consultant

Deming was a quality control expert who helped Japan, after World War II, restart their economy with the newest quality control methods. He became greatly respected and revered for his teaching and revolutionary improvements that helped to rebuild Japan.

Democritus, 460 BC–370 BC, Greek philosopher

It's interesting that Democritus, best known for his theories in physical science, had a theory about atoms and the composition of everything. He also was considered an important influence on philosophers to come.

Henri Deterding, 1866–1939, Dutch Oil founder

Richard M. DeVos, 1926–, American, co-founder of Amway, entrepreneur, and philanthropist

He and his partner, Jay Van Andel, built Amway into a large successful international company that continues to grow and prosper. He has contributed much to his resident city, Grand Rapids, Michigan. Many schools, hospitals, civic groups and public services have benefited from his philanthropy.

Charles Dickens, 1812–1870, English author

Dickens, one of the great English writers, had a very difficult early life with poverty affecting the whole family. The family was put into the debtors' prison without Charles because of his age. He visited them every Sunday until they were released. His first job was as a reporter for a local newspaper. He eventually became a prolific writer with a number of successful books. He became the most widely known English writer since Shakespeare. His very tough and difficult early years were finally rewarded. His rigid work habits allowed him to create his works which are still well known today.

Nina Disesa, American Chairperson of McCann-Erickson Worldwide Advertising agency

Walt Disney, 1901–1966, American artist, film producer, and entrepreneur

Disney was a true genius in pioneering animated cartoons (such as the magnificent *Snow White and the Seven Dwarfs*) and much more. His theme parks were also an indication of his entrepreneurial skills. His early years were very difficult and forced him to take some risks. This put him in the business of animated cartoons with his famous Mickey Mouse, followed by the rest of his cartoon characters. He won 48 Academy awards and 7 Emmys. His life was too short but what a legacy he left for us.

Benjamin Disraeli, 1804–1881, British Prime Minister and author

Disraeli was a very successful author and debater. He served in several key positions in parliament. His persistence was respected by even his adversaries. He said, "Read no history, only biographies, for that is real life, without theory."

Fyodor Dostoevsky, 1821–1881, Russian novelist

Peter Drucker, 1909–2005, Austrian born American, business author, teacher, and consultant

Drucker wrote over 35 books and was the dominant management voice of the second half of the 20th century, worldwide. He was a major influence on business management, consulting for many of the biggest and best business leaders and companies. Several of his books are classics and are still being printed and sold.

Wayne Dyer, 1940–, American self-help author and speaker

Clint Eastwood, 1930–, American actor, director and producer, Academy award winner

Clint Eastwood has a story of patience and perseverance to be admired by all of us. He was rejected in Hollywood and went to Italy where he starred in a number of very successful movies called spaghetti westerns. He was asked to come back to Hollywood and went on to star in every picture he made. He then decided he could direct and he did, winning Academy Awards. He then added producing with even more success. Most people would have been dejected early on and would never have gotten back on the road to success. Attitude, perseverance, confidence, and patience could not be better illustrated.

Thomas A. Edison, 1847–1931, American inventor and physicist

He lost much of his hearing as a boy and had little training. He worked as a newsboy and soon printed and published a small newspaper. During the Civil war he worked as a telegraph operator and invented the paper ticker tape for stock prices, which he sold to establish a research laboratory. His inventive genius produced over 1,000 patents, including the electric light bulb and a system for generating electricity. Among his many inventions was the first talking motion picture. Edison failed many times before he finally succeeded and became the great inventor that he was.

Edward VIII, 1894–1972, British monarch who abdicated the throne in 1936

The story of Edward VIII though is interesting. He was made King in January of 1936 and abdicated the throne in December 1936. Although he was popular and showed some ability to lead, he fell in love with an American divorcee and fell out of favor in England. This forced him to make a choice, England or Wallis Simpson. He chose her. He was given the title of Duke of Windsor and some unimportant duties in the Bahamas. He later settled in Paris and was never invited back to England for any official event until 1967. He died 5 years later presumably happy because he was the one who decided his fate.

Tyron Edwards, 1809–1894, American theologian

Albert Einstein, 1879–1955, German born mathematician, physicist, Nobel Prize winner

You might not think of Einstein as one to recognize the men who came before him and his contemporaries. You might think of a scientist working and thinking alone. But always teamwork comes into these efforts. It was his initiative, encouraged by his associates, to write to President Roosevelt in 1939, recommending that an initiative be made to gather all our best scientific minds to develop the atomic bomb before the Nazis in Germany did it first. This was a key decision that helped us win World War II.

Dwight David Eisenhower, 1890–1969, 34th President and Supreme Commander of all Allied forces in World War II

Eisenhower spent a lot of time as a leader, from his days in the military and then as President of the United States of America. These were two of the toughest jobs in the world and as a general and supreme leader of the armed forces he led the free world to a victory that was key to peace for the whole world.

Eisenhower was known for his honesty, humility and perseverance. His time in the military tested his ability to lead and he succeeded with a great victory in Europe. After the war he became president of Columbia University and then became the Republican candidate for president. He was elected and served two terms. These were very difficult times due to the cold war, caused by the Russia's ambitious goal to be the leading power in the world and to spread communism worldwide.

George Eliot, 1819–1880, English author

Mary Anne Evans wrote under the name of George Eliot. She was a sub-editor of the *Westminster Review*. She met George Lewes, a philosopher who was already married, and spent the next 20 years with him until he died. She wrote several novels that explored aspects of human psychology. Over the years she wrote numerous novels. As a novelist she will probably always stand among the greatest of the English school.

T. S. Eliot, 1888–1965, publisher, playwright, and literary critic

Born in St. Louis, Missouri of an old New England family, he was educated at Harvard and did graduate work at the Sorbonne in France and at Oxford in England. He became a literary editor and founded a literary journal. In 1927 he became a British citizen and also entered the Anglican Church. He was influential in poetry and its complexities. He wrote many literary pieces that were well received. Many were well known and published into volumes of his work. He received the Nobel Prize for literature.

Ralph Waldo Emerson, 1803–1882, American poet and essayist

Emerson was a writer mostly about nature and was an advocate of individualism and spiritual independence. He also was an idealist in philosophy.

Epictetus, 55–135 AD, Greek philosopher

Epictetus was a freed slave who later taught philosophy. He taught a gospel of inner freedom through self-denial, submission to providence, and the love of one's enemies. He believed that man should concern himself only with what he can control and suffer what he cannot influence. He attracted people from all over the Roman world to hear him. One of his students published his sayings and some of his discourses still exist.

Marie Eschenbach, 1830–1916, Austrian author

Euripides, 484–406 BC, Greek dramatist

Euripides wrote about 80 dramas though only 18 survived. He was known for showing people as they are, not as they ought to be.

Sam Ewing, 1920–2001, writer and humorist

Nick Faldo, 1957–, English professional golf champion

Doug Firebaugh, author, coach, and speaker

Edward L. Flom, American CEO and executive

Henry Ford, 1863–1947, American, founder of Ford Motor Company

Ford certainly was ahead of his time when he started his company in 1903 with a modern assembly line mass production operation to produce cars. He also paid his workers better than anyone else and in a sense created a customer for his cars with an energetic labor force. He resisted the labor unions because he felt he would take care of his own people better.

Jeff Foxworthy, 1958–, American comedian and TV host

Anatole France, 1844–1924, Nobel Prize winner in literature

His literary output was vast. He was chiefly known as a novelist and his scope was wide. One of his favorite subjects to write about was the transition of paganism to Christianity. In later years he became interested in social questions.

Anne Frank, 1929–1945

Anne Frank was captured with her family by the Nazis in Holland during the Second World War after they were discovered hiding in a Dutch home. She and her family were sent to a concentration camp where they all died except for the father who published the diary that Anne had written during her time in hiding. The book became a world-wide best seller and was later made into a movie. She only lived for 16 years but had great impact on the whole world. The book was translated into 50 languages. Even in this horrible situation she had some good insight about growing up.

Benjamin Franklin, 1706–1790, American statesman, diplomat, inventor, publisher, and scientist

Franklin was a remarkable person who excelled mostly as a key leader in the creation of The United States of America. He was a strong force in our struggle for freedom and independence from England. He helped draft the Declaration of Independence. He was later sent to France to negotiate their support during our Revolutionary War. Without France's support we would not have been able to win the war. He also helped form the Constitution of The United States. At the age of 83 he invented bifocal eyeglasses, one of his many inventions. He is still a household name.

Patricia Fripp, American author and speaker

Robert Fulford, 1932–, Canadian journalist and author

James A. Garfield, 1831–1881, 20th President of United States of America

Garfield was raised in poverty but managed to get a college education from Williams College, a top school then and now. He served in the civil war and was a hero in several battles leading to promotion to the rank of major general. He served in Congress for seventeen years and was unexpectedly chosen to be his party's candidate for President. He won by a narrow margin. While still in his first year as President, he was shot by a deranged man. He died two months later in 1881 at the age of 50.

Bill Gates, 1955–, Computer scientist and businessman, co-founder of Microsoft

He attended Harvard and dropped out at age 19 to start a new company with Paul Allen, his co-founder. He then sold some new software to IBM. The system became highly successful and led to great success for the company and himself, leading to enormous wealth. After several years he stepped down to establish several charitable foundations. Eventually he was leading his own large charitable foundation with the goal of worldwide help in health and educational needs. He expects to eventually give away most of his money and is partnered with Warren Buffett who has the same goals.

Harold S. Geneen, 1910–1997, American businessman, former president of ITT

Geneen took ITT from $750 million in sales to $22 billion in a period of 18 years. He also led the company to the acquisition of over 200 companies in the same 18 years. Some of the companies were Avis Rent-a-Car, Sheraton Hotels, and Hartford Fire and Life Insurance, to name a few. All of this from planned action and follow-up to guarantee success.

Malcolm Gladwell, 1963–, author of Blink and The Tipping Point

Johann Wolfgang von Goethe, 1749–1832, German author, scientist, poet, and playwright
Von Goethe was considered to be one of Europe's greatest literary figures. He was multitalented and excelled in literature and science.

Ellen Goodman, 1943–, American journalist

John Gray, 1957–, American author

Wayne Gretzky, 1961–, famous Canadian hockey player

Robert Half, American entrepreneur and human resources expert, founder of Robert Half associates

Mark Victor Hansen, 1948–, best-selling author of Chicken Soup for the Soul

Elaine Heffner, psychotherapist and author

L.L. Henderson, 1888–1957, American writer and lawyer

Heraclitus, 540–480 BC, Greek philosopher

Alan Patrick Herbert, 1890–1971, English author

George Hess, journalist

Napoleon Hill, 1883–1970, American speaker, writer, and teacher

Hill was born in Virginia and by the time he was 12 years old both his parents had died. He started writing at age 13 for a local newspaper, saving money for school. He went to law school for a short time and dropped out due to lack of funds. He was assigned to interview Andrew Carnegie, a very wealthy and powerful man. Carnegie told him that any man could achieve great success by following a simple formula. Carnegie commissioned Hill to interview 500 successful people to discover this formula and publish it. It took over 20 years to do all the interviews. Carnegie then hired him as an advisor. He published a series of books for home study. It was in 1937 that he published *Think and Grow Rich*. The book has sold over 30 million copies and still is sold everywhere.

Homer, 800–701 BC, Greek epic poet and major figure of ancient Greek literature

He was regarded in Greek and Roman antiquity as the author of the Iliad which deals with the adventurers of the Trojan War. He was thought to have been blind. His poems were written in the 8th century BC.

Tom Hopkins, American author and speaker

Horace, 65–8 BC, Roman poet and satirist

Son of a freed slave, he was Educated in Rome and Athens. He was present when Caesar was murdered and the civil war was rekindled. He joined Brutus' army and fought battles before going back to Italy. He became the unrivaled lyric poet of the time and the Poet Laureate. His work had a profound influence on poetry and literary criticism in the 17th and 18th centuries.

Jane Howard, 1923–, English novelist

Edgar Watson Howe, 1853–1937, American journalist

Aldous Huxley, 1894–1963, English critic and novelist

Born into a family that included the most distinguished members of the English ruling class, his parents and relatives were all successful in their own rights. He was respected for his skills and intellect. In his youth he was afflicted with an eye illness that nearly caused blindness. He was able to continue with school and graduated from Oxford with high honors. He had to move to California to help heal his eyes which led him to have an interest in the movies, and he became a screen writer. He published a collection of poems, got married, had an only child, and did extensive travel around the world. He loved American life and he achieved many successes. His greatest successes were in two novels, *Brave New World* and *The Doors of Perception*. He died in Los Angeles in 1963 on the same day that John F. Kennedy was assassinated.

Thomas H. Huxley, 1825–1895, English biologist

Robert Green Ingersoll, 1833–1899, American lawyer and orator.

Ingersoll served as a colonel in the Union cavalry during the Civil War and later as the attorney general of Illinois. He was also a well-known deist.

George Jackson, 1941–1971, American activist

Henry James, 1843–1916, American author

Henry James was a prolific writer and influenced many other authors. He was considered the master of the psychological novel which profoundly influenced the 20th century.

Thomas Jefferson, 1743–1826, 3rd President of United States of America

Jefferson played a key role in the formation of our new government. He drafted the Declaration of Independence that was signed on July 4, 1776. He was appointed Secretary of State by George Washington and became the Vice President to John Adams, our 2nd president. He then became our 3rd president. When he left office he returned to Virginia and founded the University of Virginia. In a strange coincidence, he and John Adams both died on the same day, the 50th anniversary of the signing of the Declaration, July 4th 1826.

Samuel Johnson, 1709–1784, English writer and critic

Spencer Johnson, English author and medical doctor

Johnson is the author of the best-selling book, *Who Moved My Cheese*, which sold millions all over the world. He also co-authored the book, *The One Minute Manager*, another best-seller. In the first book he wrote about change and how to deal with it. The second book is about performance recognition.

Vic Johnson, American author and motivational speaker

Charles "Tremendous" Jones, American speaker and teacher

Erica Jong, 1942–, American novelist

Franz Kafka, 1883–1924, Austrian author

Helen Keller, 1880–1968, American writer and crusader for the handicapped

Helen Keller's life is a remarkable story of achievement through the most difficult times. She became both deaf and blind just before turning two. She was completely unable to communicate until age seven. Her teacher, Ann Sullivan, also became famous as the one who was able to help and teach Helen. Keller was able to become a lecturer, writer, and crusader for all the handicapped. Her biography is inspirational. It's amazing to see how she was able to accomplish so much with her limitations.

John F. Kennedy, 1917–1963, 35th President of United States of America

JFK was faced with at least two major international conflicts in his shortened first term as President, and he knew very well the potential conflicts with Russia during the famous "Cold War" in the early 60s. Shortly after the East Germans, with Russian support, built a wall to separate East Berlin from the west, Kennedy had to call up, for active duty, reservists and National Guard units for deployment to Europe as a show of force. This tense situation lasted about one year and as soon as it was over, he learned that the Russians were placing missiles in Cuba. This was a far more dangerous situation and Kennedy forced Russia to remove the missiles after a dangerous face off. The risks were enormous but JFK had to take the risk since inaction would have been far more dangerous. He was assassinated in November of 1963 in Dallas, Texas. He was only 47 and showed great promise but never finished his first term as President.

Martin Luther King Jr., 1929–1968, U.S. clergyman, civil rights leader, and Nobel Peace Prize winner

He was a Baptist pastor living in Alabama when the Rosa Parks arrest sparked the bus boycott. King came to national prominence as an eloquent and courageous leader. In 1957 he founded the Southern Christian Leadership Conference. He was a brilliant orator and in 1963 led a peaceful march on Washington D.C. where he delivered his memorable "I Have a Dream" speech. He was inspired by Mahatma Gandhi and had the same philosophy of non-violence and passive resistance which proved to be instrumental in securing passage of the Civil Rights Act in 1964 and the Voting Rights Act of 1965. In 1964 he was awarded several honors including the Nobel Peace Prize. He was assassinated in 1969 in Memphis, Tenn. while on a civil rights mission. His wife Coretta Scott King has carried on his work.

Ann Landers, 1918–2002, American advice columnist

Robert Leighton, 1611–1684, Scottish prelate

Leighton was the Archbishop of Glasgow at the request of King Charles II. Leighton tried to coordinate various factions of the church with no great success.

Leonardo da Vinci, 1452–1519, Italian artist, engineer, and sculptor

Giacomo Leopardi, 1798–1837, Italian poet and writer

Elmer G. Letterman, writer

Sam Levenson, 1911–1980, American comedian

Abraham Lincoln, 1809–1865, 16th President of United States of America

We all know some things about Lincoln and his early struggles in poverty and his hard work to succeed against great odds. His skills in office as President held together a country divided. It was his behind-the-scenes ability to keep it all together that made it happen. His leadership during the Civil War may never be fully appreciated. Volumes of books have been written and few of us can appreciate the greatness of the man and his accomplishments. He is always picked as one of our greatest presidents. It's hard to imagine that more than one or two other presidents had as difficult a job.

Walter Linn

Vince Lombardi, 1913–1970, American football coach and motivator

Lombardi was a very successful coach and in demand as a motivational speaker. His greatest years were coaching the Green Bay Packers, a team that had past glories but no success for at least 14 years before he arrived as the new coach. He was a perfectionist in teaching the game and being sure that his players made few mistakes. He developed winners from players who might not have achieved that success with another team.

Henry Wadsworth Longfellow, 1807–1882, American poet

A graduate of Bowdoin College, in Maine, he spent 3 years in Europe. He held various academic positions at Bowdoin and Harvard while also visiting Europe. He had a gift of simple, romantic storytelling in verse in all the novels he wrote. He enjoyed enduring popularity with his style as a poet. Longfellow was one of the most famous poets of his time. His famous poem was "Paul Revere's Ride." You remember as most people do, "Listen my children and you shall hear, Of the midnight ride of Paul Revere . . ." It was published on the eve of the Civil War and raised the nationalism and optimistic feeling of the people by featuring the exploits of a hero and the sacrifices of brave people for freedom.

Joan Lunden, 1950–, American TV hostess and author

Niccolo Machiavelli, 1469–1527, Italian statesman, writer, and philosopher

Machiavelli held many key government positions and met many of the world's famous people. He was a keen observer of men and events. At some point he was forced to leave political life due to some problems he couldn't solve. He then turned to being a writer using what he had learned and wrote *The Prince*, his most famous book and still referred to today. It was a handbook for rulers intended to teach them how to achieve political success. His admirers praised him and his critics said he was a cynic and dangerous.

Harvey B. Mackay, 1932–, American author and successful entrepreneur

Maxwell Maltz, 1899–1995, American author and medical doctor

Orison Swett Marden, 1848–1926, American author of motivational books

Groucho Marx, 1890–1977, American comedian

William Matthews, 1942–1997, American author

Somerset Maugham, 1874–1965, English author
Somerset Maugham wrote some of the greatest classic novels of our times, *Of Human Bondage*, and *The Moon and Sixpence* are two of many. He was a very unusual man who used his real life experiences as a basis for his novels. He was a medical doctor and surgeon and secret agent in two wars and visited Tahiti and the Far East. This is just a glimpse of his life. His biography would have to read like a novel.

Charles Mayo, 1865–1939, Medical doctor who founded the Mayo Clinic
He founded the Clinic with his father and brother in 1905 in Rochester, Minn. In the years since, it has grown dramatically and become world famous. They also founded the Clinic for Education and Research in 1915. They treat multiple areas of medicine and have set a standard for other major medical clinics such as the Cleveland Clinic, in Ohio.

Charles W. Mayo, 1819–1911, born in England, lived in the United States, co-founder of the Mayo Clinic

Angela Barron McBride, American author and professor at Indiana University

Tim McCarver, 1941–, American pro baseball player and All Star catcher

Bernard Meltzer, 1916–1998, American radio advice host

H. L. Mencken, 1880–1956, American author and editor

Randy K. Milholland, comedian and writer

Robert Montgomery, 1807–1855, English poet

Thomas Moore, 1779–1852, Irish poet and composer

John Pierpont Morgan, 1837–1913, American banker, financier, art collector, entrepreneur, and philanthropist

I can still remember, even as a child, that the name J.P. Morgan meant wealth and power. He was one of America's greatest bankers and financiers and owned railroads and companies like U.S. Steel. He became a world famous art collector and, over time, gave all of his multimillion dollar collection to the Metropolitan Art Museum in New York City. He also was one of the great philanthropists, who gave away much of his fortune to charity, schools, and museums.

Mother Teresa, 1910–1997, Albanian Catholic missionary and winner of Nobel Peace prize

Mother Teresa spent her life of service in India helping the poor and dying. After teaching in a convent school, she left on her own to work in the slums of Calcutta. In 1957 she started her work with the leper colonies. She was soon joined by many more to establish hospitals and charity houses, now spread to 124 other countries. She was awarded the Pope John XXIII Peace prize in

1971 and the Nobel Peace prize in 1979. She said, "The biggest disease today is not leprosy or tuberculosis but the feeling of not being wanted."

Ogden Nash, 1902–1971, American humorist and poet

John Neal, 1793–1876, American editor, poet, novelist, and critic

Patricia Neal, 1926–2010, American actress
Patricia Neal knows something about positive attitude after recovering from a series of massive strokes. After a successful Broadway career and awards she worked in Hollywood and won an Academy Award for best actress in 1963. It was after this she became ill and made a miraculous recovery. She continued to act and was nominated for more awards. She was recognized for her recovery from the strokes and given The Heart of the Year award by President Lyndon Johnson.

Friedrich Nietzsche, 1844–1900, German philosopher

John Nordstrom, 1871–1963, founder of Nordstrom department stores
One of the main reasons for Nordstrom's success is their superb customer service and empowerment of their people to be able to make decisions without getting approval in order to satisfy a customer This empowerment is a goal for many companies now and has favorably affected the level of customer service in many of these companies.

Frank Norris, 1870–1902, American novelist

Anthony Norvell, author

P. J. O'Rourke, 1947–, American writer and satirist

Vance Packard, 1914–1997, American writer and journalist

Chuck Palahniuk, 1962–, American author

Dorothy Parker, 1879–1958, American novelist

Trey Parker, 1969–, and Matt Stone 1971–, American screenwriters

Blaise Pascal, 1623–1662, French mathematician, physicist, theologian, and writer

He was a man of many talents and had important influence in many areas of life. As a child he was a mathematical genius who contributed much to new discoveries in mathematics. He was responsible for the inventions of the barometer, hydraulic press, syringe, and a calculating machine. He also was supportive of social causes and made many other contributions.

Linus Pauling, 1901–1994, American chemist and double winner of Nobel Prize for chemistry and peace

Dr. Pauling won the Nobel Prize twice; for chemistry in 1954 and for peace in 1962. He is well known for his advocacy of vitamin C in large doses to combat multiple aliments and diseases. When he says that many ideas generate a few good ideas, I say that's good advice. Imagination is important and can generate ideas. Imagination, creativity and ideas all go together.

Norman Vincent Peale, 1898–1993, American author and famous church leader

Norman Vincent Peale was famous for his book, *The Power of Positive Thinking*, which was published in 1952 and is still in print with over 5 million copies sold. He said the book was for ordinary, plain people who had to struggle through life. The lessons taught were learned by many the hard way. He was also a very popular speaker because of the book. It was his goal to help people and apparently he did.

Mary Pettibone, American author

John J. Plomp, writer

Plutarch, 46–120 AD, Greek historian, philosopher, and biographer

Plutarch was a biographer of many famous Greek and Roman historical figures and shed light on their lives and the times they lived in. He said that there are hints about people, such as anecdotes, that are not revealed in history. He said a chance joke or remark can reveal much about a person. He contributed much to real history.

Michael Pritchard, American motivational speaker

Dan Quayle, 1941–, former Vice President of the United States

Nido Qubein, 1948–, author, consultant, and speaker

Quintilian, 35–100 AD

Daniel Raeburn, American writer

Sir Walter Raleigh, 1554–1618, English aristocrat and adventurer

He was known as an adventurer, author, poet, and navigator in the British Navy. He became a favorite of Queen Elizabeth I, and rose rapidly. He was knighted by the Queen in 1585 and became involved in the early colonization of Virginia. In 1591 he secretly married one of Elizabeth's ladies in waiting without the Queen's approval. He and his wife were sent to the Tower of London and then released. He then sought gold in the new world for England. When The Queen died in 1603, he was accused of being involved in a plot against King James I. In 1616 he was released to conduct a second expedition for gold that was unsuccessful. When he returned to England he was accused of ransacking and destroying a Spanish outpost in his travels. To appease the Spanish government he was arrested and executed in 1618. He left many poems and stories about his many adventures.

Mary Lou Retton, 1968–, 1984 Olympic Games all around women's gymnastics champion

Cardinal de Retz, 1613–1679, French Cardinal and author

Anthony Robbins, 1960–, author, speaker, and teacher

Tony Robbins has written a number of books on succeeding. He runs seminars where people learn to extend themselves and go beyond anything they ever thought they could do.

John D. Rockefeller, 1839–1937, founder of Standard Oil

He started as a clerk and then worked in a small oil refinery in Cleveland, Ohio. In 1870 he founded Standard Oil with his brother and this eventually gave him control of the U.S. oil trade. His company grew dramatically and sales and profits set records. With this enormous wealth he started to support medical research and universities. In 1913 he founded The Rockefeller Foundation to benefit mankind. He also funded the restoration of Colonial Williamsburg in Virginia.

John D. Rockefeller, Jr., 1874–1960, Chairman of the Rockefeller Institute of Medical Research

Rockefeller, an heir to the family fortune, was a philanthropist involved in giving the family fortune to worthwhile causes.

Knute Rockne, 1888–1931, American football coach at the University of Notre Dame

Rockne was one of America's most famous college football coaches and set records at Notre Dame. He also groomed his players to be better people and citizens. He was a legend and set Notre Dame apart with a reputation that is still strong. His record of 105 victories, 12 loses and 5 ties, was one of the best ever. He changed the way the game was played and in his 13 seasons his team won 3 national championships with 5 undefeated seasons. His life ended in a tragic plane crash in 1931 at the young age of 43.

Will Rogers, 1879–1935, American cowboy, actor, and humorist

Born in Oklahoma in Indian Territory, he led an adventurous life with travels to South America and South Africa. He worked in varied Wild West shows in the U.S.A. and overseas. In 1905 he was doing skilled roping acts which led to a career in acting that started on Broadway and ended in the movies. He was known for his folksy wisdom and jokes that poked fun at most everything, especially the government. He was one of the world's best known celebrities. He made 71 movies and wrote over 4,000 syndicated newspaper columns. He became the leading political wit and a top paid movie actor. In 1935 he took a trip with his best friend, Wiley Post, in a small plane on a trip to Alaska. The plane crashed and both men were killed. He used to joke about his epitaph and what it should say. He wanted it to read, "I joked about every prominent man of my time, but I never met a man I didn't like." He said he was so proud of this, ". . . that I can hardly wait to die, so it can be carved."

Jim Rohn, 1930–2009, American author and speaker

Mickey Rooney, 1920–, American actor

Eleanor Roosevelt, 1884–1962, former first lady of 32nd President

She was active in many social causes that had impact on the country. She was our representative to the U.N. General Assembly, was an opponent of child labor, and campaigned for minimum wages.

F.D. Roosevelt, 1882–1945, 32nd President of U.S.A.

He was a distant cousin of Teddy Roosevelt and was born into a wealthy family. He was well educated and became a lawyer who was admitted to the bar in New York, then served as a state senator and asst. secretary of the Navy. During this time he was stricken with polio and paralyzed in his legs. He was elected governor of New York and then defeated Hoover to become our 32nd president in 1932. He was faced with very poor economic conditions—The Great Depression of 1933. This is why he introduced the "New Deal" and Social Security in 1935. He was then reelected in 1936 to a second presidential term followed by a third term in 1940 and finally a fourth term in 1944. He was the first and last president to exceed two terms. He joined with the Allied Forces during the Second World War when Japan attacked the U.S.A. in 1941. The combined Allied Forces won a great victory in1945. Sadly Roosevelt died in 1945, three weeks before the war ended in Europe.

Theodore Roosevelt, 1858–1919, 26th President of United States, author, and Nobel Peace Prize winner

Roosevelt was an avid hunter and outdoorsman who was very action oriented. He served as Governor of New York State, Vice President, and President. He accomplished much domestically and internationally including construction of the Panama Canal and improving our military. He is known for his words "Speak softly and carry a big stick." He was awarded the Nobel peace prize in 1906.

J.K. Rowling, 1965–, English author of the Harry Potter series.

She began her career as a teacher of English and French. Her first published book was Harry Potter and the Philosopher's

Stone—earlier books were rejected by numerous publishers—and it was an immediate success. This was followed by six more Harry Potter books, all equally successful, and seven blockbuster movies. All in all they made her the wealthiest woman in England and winner of several awards, including the British Book Awards Children's Book of the Year prize for 1999.

Rita Rudner, 1953–, American comedian

John Ruskin, 1819–1900, English author and art critic

Bertram Russell, 1872–1970, British Author and Nobel Prize winner for literature
Russell was a controversial figure, multitalented, and not always on the side of public opinion. He was married four times. He wrote a book on philosophy *The Problems of Philosophy*, which can still be read as a brilliant introduction to the subject. Politics became his dominant concern during WWI and his extreme pacifism led to imprisonment where he wrote more about mathematics. Afterwards, he earned a living by giving lectures and writing. The rise of fascism led him to renounce his pacifism in 1939. He returned to England from abroad after WWII and was honored with a few awards including the Nobel Prize for literature in 1950. His biggest contributions were in philosophy, mathematics, and writing.

Antoine de Saint-Exupery, 1900–1944, French writer and aviator

George Santayana, 1863–1952, Spanish philosopher, poet, and novelist

William Saroyan, 1908–1981, American author
Saroyan, a successful and prolific writer, turned down the Pulitzer Prize for his play The Time of Your Life.

Max Sarton

Marilyn vos Savant, 1946–, American columnist and writer

Charles Schwab, 1937–, American entrepreneur and stock trader

Albert Schweitzer, 1875–1965, Alsatian philosopher, theologian, physician, musician, and winner of the Nobel Peace Prize

He committed different times of his life to his many interests and in midlife decided to become a doctor and surgeon. Then he went to Africa to set up a hospital and clinic with his own money. He used the proceeds from his concerts and lectures to equip and maintain the hospital. He also set up a leper colony. In 1952 he was awarded the Nobel Peace Prize. He was a man of multiple talents and skills who chose to sacrifice many years in service to his fellow man. He has been called one of the greatest Christians of all time.

Haile Selassie, 1892–1975, Emperor of Ethiopia in the early 1930s

Seneca, 5 BC–65 AD, Roman politician and philosopher

Marcus Annaeus Seneca, 55 BC–40 AD, Roman rhetorician

Known as Seneca the Elder, he was born in Cordoba, Spain and educated in Rome where he lived. He wrote a history of Rome which was lost over time. He also wrote a collection of imaginary court cases for his sons to learn. He was the father of Lucius Annaeus Seneca, who became known as Seneca the Younger and became the tutor of the future Emperor Nero of Rome.

Dr. Seuss (Theodore Seuss Geisel), 1904–1991, American author and cartoonist

William Shakespeare, 1564–1616, English playwright and author

Shakespeare was considered England's greatest dramatist.

Cathy Shaw, 1959–, American comedian and author

George Bernard Shaw, 1856–1950, Irish playwright and author, won the Noble Prize for Literature.

Shaw's early life was full of struggles and poverty. His first five novels were rejected. He turned to socialism and wrote many socialist tracts. He also became a drama and music critic. After this period he turned to playwriting. His reputation began to grow in England and abroad. He covered a wide range of topics from politics to family life. Two of his best-selling plays were *Androcles* and *The Lion and Pygmalion*—later to become *My Fair Lady*, which also became a hit movie and prize winner. He was awarded the Nobel Prize for literature in 1925.

John Sladek, 1938–2000, American author

Hannah Whitall Smith, 1832–1911, American author

Ralph W. Sockman, 1889–1970, author

Socrates, 409–399 BC, Greek philosopher

He fought in the Peloponnesian War. He wrote nothing, founded no schools, and had no formal disciples but is known, with Plato and Aristotle, as one of the three great figures in ancient philosophy. The principal source of knowledge about his life comes from Plato. He was tried at the age of 70 for corrupting the youth and for impiety. He rejected the option of merely paying a fine, declined a later opportunity to escape, and was sentenced to die by drinking hemlock.

Solon, 638–559 BC, Athenian law giver

Solon was a great contributor to our laws. Born into an aristocratic family, he was appointed to reform the constitution. He set free all slaves who had been enslaved by debt, reformed the currency, and repealed stringent laws.

Thomas Sowell, 1930–, American writer and economist

Herbert Spencer, 1820–1903, English author and philosopher

Gloria Steinem, 1934–, American feminist and publisher

Henry L. Stimson, 1867–1950, American politician

Henry Stimson served under four presidents including F. D. R. Roosevelt and Harry S. Truman during World War II. His leadership and advice were important to these two presidents and helped in winning the war. His influence was decisive in leading President Truman to use the atomic bomb against Japan in World War II.

W. Clement Stone, 1902–2002, American businessman, philanthropist, and author

His father died when Clement was 3, leaving his family impoverished due to his father's gambling losses. When he was 6 he sold newspapers and at 13 owned his own newsstand. At age 16 he joined his mother in opening an insurance agency. He was an avid reader of the Horatio Alger stories where poor boys overcame adversity to reach success. He was greatly influenced by Napoleon Hill's book, *Think and Grow Rich*. He made millions in the insurance business and eventually helped others to succeed. He also wrote an autobiography about his early years and lessons learned. By 1930 he had over 1,000 insurance agents selling insurance and a company with over one billion in assets. He always said one of the most important days in his life was when he started to read, *Think and Grow Rich*. He also said that the Bible was the world's greatest self-help book. He preached that a positive mental attitude is necessary for achieving worthwhile success.

C. Neil Strait, 1934–2003, clergyman and author

George Sweeting, author

Jonathan Swift, 1667–1745, Anglo-Irish satirist and clergyman

He was a novelist during his years of political involvement but he always went back to writing. In 1726 he wrote *Gulliver's Travels*. This was a satire on politics and religion that became very popular—maybe his most successful book. He was a champion for many causes and tried to help the lower class in their constant struggles.

Charles Swindoll, 1934–, American radio clergyman and author

Publilius Syrus, 100 BC, Italian Saint

Margaret Thatcher, 1925–, former Prime Minister of England.

Margaret Thatcher, famous and able, also had a sense of humor. She managed in a difficult job with the patience she needed. She was enormously successful in a difficult time as the prime minister. She was the first woman to serve as prime minister and served from 1979 to 1990, longer than anyone in the previous 150 years.

Clarence Thomas, 1948–, American Supreme Court Justice

Henry David Thoreau, 1817–1862, American essayist and poet

He started as a teacher and in 1839 began his walks and studies in nature which became his main occupation. He built a shanty in the woods by Walden Pond where he wrote many of his essays and the classic *Walden*, or *Life in the Woods*. The rest of his writings were published after his death. He kept a daily journal of his walks and observations from which 30 volumes were published.

Count Leo Tolstoy, 1828–1910, Russian writer and philosopher

Brian Tracy, 1944–, Canadian author, consultant, speaker, and teacher

Calvin Trillen, 1935–, American columnist

Harry S. Truman, 1884–1972, 33rd President of the United State of America

Truman was an outspoken man who took over for President Franklin Roosevelt, who died unexpectedly on April 12, 1945. Truman will likely go down in history as one of our best presidents because of the critical and crucial decisions he had to make at the end of World War II and during the world wide recovery after the war. He told it as it is and was famous for saying "The buck stops here."

Mark Twain, 1835–1910, American humorist, journalist, and author

Mark Twain was a popular personality, great writer, and observer. In his early years he bounced around from job to job. He used his experiences as the basis for much of his writing. He seemed to be a poor business man, though, always failing in one venture after another and always recouping by writing and lecturing. On a trip to England in 1867, he wrote, *The Prince and the Pauper*, one of his greatest successes, and *A Connecticut Yankee* in *King Arthur's Court*. His two masterpieces, *The Adventures of Tom Sawyer* and *The Adventures of Huckleberry Finn*, are based on his boyhood experiences.

Paul Valery, 1871–1945, French poet and critic

Abigail Van Buren (Pauline Phillips), 1918–, American advice columnist

Henry Van Dyke, 1852–1933, American author and clergyman

Gore Vidal, 1925–, American writer

Voltaire, 1694–1778, French writer and historian
Voltaire achieved early success and became known for his satirical work. It was this satire that got him in trouble from time to time and he was imprisoned on some of those occasions. He found it necessary to move from one country to another, as his satirical writings angered several powerful people. He was one of the inspirations for the French Revolution. He was a champion of the people and was considered the embodiment of the 18th century Enlightenment. He was eventually invited back to Paris and died there at age 84.

Charles Wadsworth, musician

Denis Waitley, 1933–, American author and speaker

Sam Walton, 1918–1992, American entrepreneur and founder of Wal-Mart
Sam Walton knew the value and the power of the customer. He was an early leader in discount retailing and a pioneer in the use of computers to manage inventory and profit margins. He inspired his employees and they benefited from the enormous growth in their company stock.

William Arthur Ward, 1921–1994, American author of inspirational books

George Washington, 1732–1799, 1st president of the United States of America

He was an immigrant from England. His grandfather acquired wealth and position in Virginia. George's father died when he was a boy and in 1752 he inherited the Mt. Vernon estate. At that time he was appointed head of the local militia in Virginia to fight the French. Under British General, Edward Braddock, Washington served with the rank of Colonel. He was put in charge of all military forces in Virginia when Braddock was killed. In 1759 he married Martha Custis, a wealthy young woman, and this made them one of the wealthiest families in Virginia. He entered politics and represented Virginia in the Continental Congress. He was the inevitable choice to be Commander in Chief of the Revolutionary army in 1775. After many military reverses, the surrender of the British ended the War of Independence. Washington resigned his commission to return home to Virginia. In 1789 was elected first President of the United States of America. In 1793 he was elected to a second term. He retired in 1797 to allow John Adams to run for the presidency. Washington died in 1799 at Mt. Vernon.

Martha Washington, 1732–1802, wife of the 1st president of the United States

Bill Watterson, 1958–, American cartoonist

Rev. John Wesley, 1707–1788, English minister

Mae West, 1892–1980, famous movie star

Mae West was a big star in her time. She was known for her glamour and wit. She wrote many of the scripts for her shows and movies. She appeared in her last movie in 1970. She starred with Cary Grant in his first movie. The inflatable life vest was named after her, "the Mae West."

John Wicker, American

Oscar Wilde, 1854–1900, Irish playwright, novelist, essayist, poet, and wit

Bud Wilkinson, 1916–1994, American college football coach
Bud Wilkinson was a legendary Hall of Fame football coach at the University of Oklahoma.

Bern Williams, 1929–2003, English writer and philosopher

Woodrow T. Wilson, 1856–1924, 28th President of United States of America
Wilson was president of Princeton University, governor of New Jersey, and was then elected to the Presidency. At the end of World War I he played a key role in a peace plan leading to the Armistice. He proposed a League of Nations, which was rejected by the Senate and may have led to Wilson's stroke and illness which eventually ended his career. He served two terms. He was awarded the Noble Peace Prize in 1919.

P. G. Wodehouse, 1881–1975, English novelist and wit

Thomas Wolfe, 1900–1938, American author
Thomas Wolfe, in his short life, wrote several best-selling and important novels.

John Wooden, 1910–2010, American championship basketball coach at UCLA
He coached UCLA to a record eleven championships. Beyond his coaching skills was his success at developing character in his players.

William Wordsworth, 1770–1850, English poet

William of Wykeham, 1324–1404, English churchman and statesman

William of Wykeham is known as the founder and father of public schools in England.

William Butler Yeats, 1865–1939, Irish poet and winner of the Nobel Prize for literature

About the Authors

Joel Weiss, a seasoned executive and manager with more than fifty years of experience in business, also served as a major in the Air Force, and is the author of *How To Get From Cubicle To Corner Office* and *The Quotable Manager*. He holds a BS and MBA in management from Rutgers University and resides with his family in Ada, Michigan.

John Weiss shares with his father a great interest in quotes for their unique value to motivate, educate and entertain. John has a B.A. in business management from Florida State University. He lives with his wife and works in Charlotte, NC.

ABOUT THE PUBLISHER

Familius was founded in 2012 with the intent to align the founders' love of publishing and family with the digital publishing renaissance which occurred simultaneous with the Great Recession. The founders believe that the traditional family is the basic unit of society, and that a society is only as strong as the families that create it.

Familius' mission is to help families be happy. We invite you to participate with us in strengthening your family by being part of the Familius family. Go to www.familius.com to subscribe and receive information about our books, articles, and videos.

Website: www.familius.com

Facebook: www.facebook.com/paterfamilius

Twitter: @familiustalk

Pinterest: www.pinterest.com/familius